No CoMFoRT ZoNE

No CoMFoRT ZoNE

Notes on Living with Post Traumatic Stress Disorder

Marla Handy

Mocassa
Press

Editor: Mary Anne Mulligan

Cover and Interior Design: Julie Raasch

Mocassa Press, PO Box 45355, Madison, WI 53744, USA

www.mocassapress.com

Publish date: December, 2010

ISBN: 978-0-9831111-0-8

This book is dedicated to everyone who believes that she or he is the only one. You're not.

Contents

So

This is not a memoir. I don't know you well enough for that.

In fact, I'm not sure I know my own past well enough for that.

This is about my today, my every day. I want you to know something about what it's like to live my life. I often don't react to life's events like most of you, and the roots of my reactions aren't obvious.

I have post-traumatic stress disorder (PTSD), a condition most often associated with war veterans. Unfortunately, it is also prevalent here on the home front, among those of us who have seen the really ugly side of life: sex abuse, rape, captivity, exploitation, the threat of harm to loved ones. We become damaged in the same way. It just tends to take us longer to get diagnosed.

My condition is the result of experiencing an extreme, but very real, slice of humanity. The consequences are lasting. I'm writing this because I want you to know me and my messiness and, as a result, know that you also come in contact with this slice of humanity. You live among those who create the messiness, and those of us who are marked by it. Ugliness is not confined to sensational news stories and hushed gossip. It wanders through our daily lives, but those of you with a choice often do not see it.

I don't have that choice.

I see it. Or sense it. Or fear it. And sometimes I react in ways that are hard to explain and even embarrassing. This is what I always considered to be my messiness.

It took me years to figure out that it is PTSD.

I don't know you well enough to tell you all the gritty details of my life, but I do want you to know me better. And I want you to know what I've learned about PTSD.

This isn't a self-help book. I don't claim to have any answers or magic wands. All I have to offer is a window into one life. But maybe a glimpse through this window, framed by an understanding of PTSD, will make it easier to recognize this kind of messiness when you see it.

And that would make me feel less alone.

But then, feeling isolated is a symptom of PTSD.

🝔 🝔 🝔

Trauma, by definition, is horrifying and to some extent disrupts the lives of any who experience it. But, for some of us, trauma permanently alters our being. Our biology and emotional reactions to the world are changed in measurable, physical ways.

It pushes us through the looking glass.

This is post-traumatic stress disorder. The symptoms include reexperiencing the traumatic event(s) in different ways, hyperarousal that can take various forms, avoidance of things that are associated with the event(s) and feelings of emotional numbness. Other symptoms can include suicidal thoughts or substance abuse. It often comes with a sense of shame or guilt for either not having prevented the trauma or surviving it when others did not.

Although those of us with PTSD may also have depression at times, PTSD is not the same as depression. In fact, it is classified as an anxiety disorder, one that can forever change how the body reacts to the world.

PTSD is now believed to come in two flavors, regular and complex. These are separate from the categories of acute (symptoms lasting six months or less) and chronic (symptoms lasting more than six months, often a lifetime).

"Regular" PTSD is usually the result of experiencing a single traumatic event or episode such as a rape, a car accident, a natural disaster or witnessing a murder. The trauma of these events includes the very real belief that one might not survive. Most soldiers who have PTSD have this type. Even though they may have experienced traumatic stress over the length of their deployment, the trauma was still isolated from their "real" lives.

People with regular PTSD just want to get back to where they were, to what was once their real life. When they could relax. When they were innocent.

They wish they didn't know now what they didn't know then.

Those with complex post-traumatic stress disorder (C-PTSD) have lost more than their sense of safety or control in the world. Their sense of personhood and personal integrity has also been violated or stunted. People with C-PTSD either never had a "then" — a time before things got bad — or their earlier experience was overcome by having "real" life become continuously traumatic. This applies to people who have been under the complete control of others for an extended period of time. Captives, hostages, kids trapped in sex rings, POWs, those caught in life-threatening domestic abuse situations and victims of childhood abuse and sexual abuse usually fall into this category.

People with complex post-traumatic stress disorder not only have symptoms of PTSD, which can be very confusing, but they're also not quite sure of their own identities, because the trauma crushed their sense of being an individual with a right to choice and expression.

Traumatic events might shatter one's sense of continuity in the world, but continuously conforming to the demands of an oppressor can shatter one's sense of continuity as a person. When this sort of trauma happens to kids, they can have a hard time developing a solid sense of personhood at all. They don't lose themselves because they never formed a cohesive sense of self.

When people with either type of PTSD have a "before" to reference, they may never be exactly who they were before the trauma, but they know they did function at one point. They know they have that capacity. They may be scattered all over the place, but they know that all the parts are there.

Kids who grew up with no "before" reference may not even know what parts they need, so they make them up as they go along. They don't know how to "just be yourself." That sense of making it up comes with the insecurity of being found lacking on a very deep level. And with that comes the potential of very deep shame.

Complex PTSD is not yet an officially accepted diagnosis, which means experts in the field have not agreed upon diagnostic criteria, so insurance companies won't pay for its treatment. For the time being, people who exhibit symptoms beyond those identified for PTSD and not otherwise categorized, can be diagnosed with the lovely term DESNOS: Disorders of Extreme Stress Not Otherwise Specified.

❧ ❧ ❧

I am officially diagnosed with chronic PTSD, but strongly relate to some aspects of complex PTSD.

Mine wasn't just a run-of-the-mill dysfunctional family. The quick and dirty story is that my mother was often psychotic and was diagnosed as schizophrenic. My father was never officially diagnosed with anything other than gout. But, at a minimum, he was a nasty alcoholic. For me, my psychotic mother was the safer and more stable parent.

I experienced unpredictable abuse and neglect. I was sexually abused as a very young child. I was terrorized by my father for a number of years. And I experienced a life-threatening assault and rape by a stranger when I was in my early twenties.

This is not a justification for my condition, but an explanation. Seeing this in writing helps. It reminds me that I'm not just an oversensitive wimp, and almost convinces me that my remnants of shame are unwarranted.

Almost.

Comfort and Fear

Our comfort zone. It's safe. It's reliable. It's anxiety-neutral. By definition, it doesn't challenge. It's shuffling around the house in slippers on a rainy afternoon. It's default mode.

For the most part, we're not even aware of it until we near its edges. But sometimes we reach the border and make a quick dash over it for entertainment's sake. We scare ourselves for fun, for the adrenaline rush. We tell ghost stories over a campfire. We tentatively make our way through a dark haunted house, giggling in nervous anticipation of a jolt to our system.

We wait in long boring lines in exchange for a few minutes of screaming hysteria as we drop off the edge of the earth on a roller coaster. We read horror stories and pay to see the latest slasher movie.

Fear as entertainment is a vacation from the predictable. We enjoy it because it's temporary. When it's over, life will be as it was.

Then there are the excursions from our comfort zone that are meant to test us and, ultimately, expand the range of our ease. Sometimes we're forced into these settings and sometimes we feel honored to be invited. Working with people who seem weird to us, giving a speech, feeling so uncomfortable hearing a casual racial slur that we *have* to say something, even if it is socially awkward. These things push.

Others things pull. Good teachers, the mysteries of another culture, the pursuit of a childhood dream. These trips aren't meant to allow us to go back to life as it was. They are meant to change our perceptions of ourselves and our lives and, perhaps, to expand our comfort zone to include more of the unpredictable. Ropes courses, leadership seminars and diversity workshops are deliberate pulls. They are designed so participants can challenge their assumptions about themselves and the world. A fear is confronted and we gain confidence in a larger arena.

I sense that most people have comfort zones; these big cushy bubbles they live in. Sometimes they take little vacations from them as entertainment; sometimes they push their limits to become something new or stand for something bigger than themselves.

All these steps are admired to some degree. In fact, not taking them is seen as at least a tad shameful. Not willing to ride the roller coaster or watch a horror film? Forgivable, but you're still a bit of a party pooper.

But what about when someone is faced with a real-life horror? The world wants to see them as brave, either through stoic acceptance or a transformational learning experience. How many cancers are "bravely fought" and add new meaning to life? How many amputees fight back to a near-normal life and live with a newfound appreciation for their intact abilities? When something awful happens, we want to see the warrior emerge. We find inspiration and, therefore, comfort in those who have overcome huge obstacles.

Those of us with cancer, who have been raped, or who have endured domestic violence aren't called victims anymore. We're called survivors. It's supposed to be more empowering, which is supposed to help us move forward. We've been rebranded as people whose horrors have somehow focused and strengthened us. Survivors, after all, have found a cause outside themselves, or a heartbeat within themselves, that directs their moment-to-moment existence. They may have their doubts and continuing struggles, but they move forward. To everyone's relief.

Sorry, but this does not fit for me. I've been victimized. I know that I'm supposed to consider myself a survivor, because I'm so "high functional," but I don't. It's too soon to tell and I suspect it will always be too soon to tell. I could have easily ended up as a homeless woman who wears her underwear outside her jeans — and I'm afraid I still could. I have a warm place in my heart for such women. They're human. They count.

And I have a problem with that moving forward thing.

By definition, PTSD is past-oriented and people with PTSD often have a foreshortened sense of the future. I know I could die at any minute, or the apocalypse could be in the very next frame. So what's left? Now and the past. The most intense aspects of my past were shit. They were powerful enough to rewire my brain so that my now is a little unpredictable, too.

❧ ❧ ❧

So how does one live with that? My now has been a matter of moving, in some direction, trying to escape the pile of shit attached to me. My strategy, until a few years ago, was to keep my shit beautifully packaged. I viewed it as a large box covered with handmade paper, tied to me with cotton string. Others found it interesting, but it slowed me down.

On the wrapping paper were lovely handwritten narratives of what was inside. The handwriting was very small, however, so I had to let people come close to read it. "There was the time when I believed my dad was going to kill me by slamming me against a wall, choking me, and forcing me to tell him that he was smarter than me." "There was the time my mother believed I was a witch and knew all of the answers to her problems. But then she changed and thought she was the Virgin Mary and didn't recognize me anymore. She signed into the psych ward that way."

I have always had interesting stories to tell about my life, but I'm careful about introducing them. Not everyone can handle them. Those who can't, pull back. Sometimes kindly, sometimes with obvious vulnerability of their own, sometimes dismissively.

Those who have accepted the facts of my life often find me admirable for surviving, even thriving, in spite of it all.

You might think I would find that comforting, but I never have. It creates, or emphasizes, the distance between us. They see triumph over past obstacles, whereas I experience the continuing vulnerability of walking a tightrope. There is no point of completion, no sigh of relief, no victory dance in the end zone.

To me, my life has been defined by vulnerability. My greatest achievements have only been efforts to prove to myself that I'm not a wimp. My moments of deepest shame have been when I've been overpowered by others, or by my own neediness.

Even after achieving a level of stability in my life as an adult, little things would happen that would leave this "professionally respected, world-traveling" woman collapsed sobbing, shaking and cowering in a corner. I would emerge disoriented, emotionally spent, confused about the intensity of my feelings and really, really ashamed. Why would this happen? I mean, I had had plenty of therapy. I seemed to be doing well. Had I actually flunked? If so, I was quite the fraud because people would comment on my strength. Was I really, deep down, crazy? Given my mother's history, this thought was terrifying.

These were flashbacks, a symptom of PTSD, but I didn't know it. I now recognize them, and that does help. I understand what's happened, which provides some logic to the experience, and that makes me feel less crazy. It does not, however, make the flashbacks feel less random. And I have chronic PTSD, which means it's not going away. Although I'll continue to learn to manage and live with it, I still know that I could be yanked back to that hellhole at any moment. That fear is a part of my days, my nights, myself.

* * *

I awake every morning engulfed in a familiar fog. I come to consciousness and am at several different ages at once. I am three, I am eight, I am thirteen. Those ages were unhappy times. Each contains a moment of horror that I sometimes relive through random flashbacks. My past is not a solid foundation upon which I stand to face each day. It's a surface of wavering, uneven layers of memories and vulnerability that greets me each morning. I open my eyes and simultaneously sort through it all and make sure it's in order. Things may have moved, but they're all here. I made it through the night. I step on this shifting surface and find my balance, anew. Again. Okay, time for coffee.

* * *

I react to the world as I do because I've had my personal safety violated, which also makes me the type of victim that many need to call survivors. Otherwise, we make them uncomfortable.

They need us to move on, to be heroic, so they can be inspired and comforted by the acceptable ending to our saga. Recognizing that someone may be living in a continuous state of injury is too depressing and makes them feel powerless. And feeling powerless is scary.

But the fear of powerlessness is different than fear as entertainment or the fear of reaching out to expand one's sense of competency in the world. This is the type of fear that invades and dissolves your comfort zone, leaving you bare and vulnerable. It's terrifying.

Powerlessness is not a state that many people choose to stay in for very long, so they move away from it. They explicitly or silently tell those who are injured or grieving to hurry on to the hero, or at least the stoic, stage. Get up. Get over it. Get on with it.

"Hey, sorry for your problems but don't let this change *my* life or *my* sense of safety."

But that momentary terror of powerlessness? It's just a whiff of what it's like to live with post-traumatic stress disorder. Because, with PTSD, there is no comfort zone. Ever.

Randomness and Routine

Post-traumatic stress disorder is both a result of randomness and a source of it. It is a conditioned reaction to living in terror of the next horrible event. It also creates apparently random physical and emotional reactions to routine life events. You can't trust the world and you can't make sense of your reactions to it. Nothing fits together in a logical pattern.

It's enough to make you think you're crazy.

As a child, our family often appeared normal to the outside world and, in fact, great effort was put into pulling that off. But I grew up with the distinct understanding that there was the outside world, and then there was home.

The familiarity of our house had a certain level of comfort, but it also meant being on guard. I could never quite relax because incomprehensible and excruciatingly painful things happened at random.

At the breakfast table one morning, my father ended a seemingly calm discussion with my mother by throwing a cup of scalding hot coffee into the face of my younger sibling, who was sitting in a high chair next to him. He never even looked at the baby. As my mother jumped up to care for their screaming child, he said something to the effect of, "I told you I was done talking about this," and walked off.

I felt guilty because I hadn't been paying enough attention to stop this from happening. We were all supposed to watch out for the baby. I knew that.

I was eight or nine.

❡ ❡ ❡

A key element of PTSD is living in constant anticipation of the next bad thing. The technical term for this is hypervigilance. It's an over-the-top awareness of any possible sign of impending chaos.

Chris Rock does a wonderful piece about always being on guard for racism that explains hypervigilance perfectly. He says he could be sitting down with Regis Philbin doing an interview about his latest movie, a kid's cartoon show in which he does the voice of a zebra, and Regis could pull out a pencil, stab Chris in the neck and say "take that, ya fuckin' nigger!" And Chris's response would be "I should have seen it coming."

❧   ❧   ❧

Alfred Hitchcock said, "There is no terror in the bang, only in the anticipation of it." That may be true for movies. In real life, for those of us with PTSD, the bangs are as bad as the unrelenting anticipation. The bangs are a measure of how bad things could get. After awhile, a line was crossed and I, like Chris Rock, knew that anything was possible.

Being hypervigilant is like being trapped in a haunted house, always anticipating a shock.

The anticipation is so high that even minor events can cause a major jolt. A clanging pot or a coaster falling to the floor can cause me to jump and gasp. It happens at home, mostly, but once I cowered in a grocery store line when the conveyor belt started and caused a bottle to topple.

The woman behind me kindly put her hand on my shoulder and said, "It's okay."

I know that jumping at little things makes no sense. Doing so in public is embarrassing. But there is no decision involved. I can't stop myself. It's as if my body lives in a parallel universe. This is called an exaggerated startle response and is so deeply rooted that it is rarely relieved, no matter how well PTSD treatment goes.

On the other hand, the exaggerated startle response is the basis of the only source of humor I've ever found in PTSD:

Why will there never be a "Race for the Cure" for PTSD? Because the starting pistol would cause half the runners to hit the ground in panic.

Okay, so I'm no Chris Rock.

Past and Present

So I have a bad case of nerves. Why can't I just get on with life? If you're wondering about that at this point, I understand. I've asked that question most of my life.

As I've come to know myself and PTSD better, I've realized that I can't just get over the bad things that happened to me because, well, they aren't over. They've become ingrained in my being and I'm still living them as I live my present life. It's like living life on a split-screen television. One section is my present, in which I go about my life as a professional, middle-aged, middle-class white American woman with a Ph.D. On the other side is the past, a montage of clips from my childhood, the theme of which changes and may or may not relate specifically to what is happening on the current side of the screen at any given moment. The line that splits the screen is not static. Sometimes it crowds my past into a narrow strip that hums and flashes but rarely distracts from my current life. Sometimes it crowds my current life into a mere thread just wide enough for my next breath.

It's usually somewhere between those extremes, but it's exhausting to live two or more lives at once.

❧   ❧   ❧

Everyone has memories of good and bad times and can voluntarily call up some of them, then set them aside again and live in the present. Some people dwell in the past out of choice or habit. They may relive their glory days or cultivate a past hurt. This may even get in the way of their current happiness.

But this is not the same as having intrusive thoughts of traumatic events or reexperiencing them.

Now, whatever you do, do not think about a pink elephant.

So, what did you just picture? A pink elephant. You've had people do this with you before. I just planted an intrusive thought in your mind. Now, imagine that pink elephant popping into your mind every five to ten seconds. Imagine coming to wakefulness in the morning and, in that split second before you open your eyes, you see pink elephants and wonder if they are in the room.

For me, the pink elephants are a part of life.

Sometimes they are just irritating distractions, like a song stuck in my head. Sometimes they are more real than my current surroundings. Sometimes I can't even read, not with the roar of a herd of stampeding pink elephants throbbing in my brain.

The elephants are constant, uninvited companions. Much like hypervigilance, these intrusive thoughts are unrelenting. They are the past that is always there. When they start to squeeze out the current side of the screen, taking over much more of my consciousness, they're worse. It becomes hard to keep up with my moment-to-moment present, much less absorb new information. Everyday life becomes an onslaught of demands I can barely manage.

*   *   *

I have a current life full of relationships and responsibilities. Maintaining it takes energy, focus and an ability to be present. When the past swells and presses against the present, it takes an incredible amount of effort to contain it enough that I can do the minimum required in my current day-to-day life.

At those times, it's hard to contain and it's hard to explain.

I recently saw a dear friend who I've known for almost 30 years. She has seen me at my best and at my almost-worst. We were catching up over coffee at her condo overlooking Lake Michigan. We're in our fifties. We have notable jobs, life partners, changing bodies and fluctuating retirement plans. We talk and then get to the real question . . . so how *are* you?

And I found myself talking about the time when I was thirteen and my dad decided I hadn't dried the dishes well enough. He removed my pillow from its pillowcase and replaced it with all the flatware from the drawers and all the chopping knives. He put this sack of randomly sharp hardware at the top of my bed, ordered me to put my head on it and said I needed to sleep that way all night. He would keep my door open and check periodically to make sure I hadn't cheated and moved off the metal. Of course, I was terrorized and awake all night.

My friend kept her eyes on me, without blinking, and then asked, "So how are you doing with all that?"

How do I answer that? It's more than 40 years after the fact, yet this is the most pressing emotional issue of my life right now. It seeps into my days and floods me with fear.

I looked at her and felt the gulf of both time and experience. I felt ashamed, even though this is a friend who wouldn't shame me. I also felt very alone. Somehow there must be a way to integrate my then and now, but I haven't found it. I was comforted to know that this sliver of my current life, this friend, would not be pushed away by my past, but I couldn't really meet her in the present, either. We just trust that we will again at some point.

❦ ❦ ❦

Somewhere between swamping the present with the past and punctuating it with exaggerated startle responses are triggers. Triggers can be specific or general. They are sensations — a sound, a smell, a sight — that suddenly yank me back to the past. There is a cause-and-effect relationship that snaps into play but can't always be explained. I may have no clue why I'm suddenly cowering and confused or I may know that X always seems to set me off. It may make no sense though because I can't remember the original event that sparked the trigger. Or, the anxiety around the original event may have become so generalized that seemingly unrelated items or events can set off a response.

Fortunately, my responses to triggers haven't been dangerous to myself or others, unlike those of many combat vets who were trained to react violently in self-defense. My responses may terrify and humiliate me but, to others, they just make me quirky. I tell myself to get used to it. So far I haven't.

For example, I have a thing about boxes and miscellaneous junk left in the hallways of my home. This trigger was a surprise for me and caused major emotional spikes before I realized why it was so disturbing.

They blocked my way. They made me feel trapped. I was going to get raped and couldn't escape.

I know it's a huge illogical leap from, "There are boxes in the hall" to "I'm about to be raped," but that's my emotional reality. I remind myself that it's illogical, which is somewhat calming, but often not enough. So, the people I live with (and who love me) take care to remove what have become known as "the scary boxes in the hall." We've determined that, if I don't have a three-foot clearance, I start to get edgy. Edgy may be manageable, if uncomfortable, but it depletes my emotional reserves. So, if a glass is dropped and shattered, or the cats spring into a fight, I may catapult from a startle to a flashback. So we try to manage my space.

❧   ❧   ❧

I also have a thing about spots and splatters.

Mustard and other yellowish things are bad. I've always known the source of that trigger, however. One day when I was five or six I was eating something and got mustard on my white shirt. It caused a lot of screaming from the adults around me. I tried to wipe it off, but that caused more screaming and I had my arms yanked to the side. It seems I also had mustard on my fingers so, instead of cleaning my shirt, I was just smearing it.

The shirt wasn't mine. It was my cousin's. My mother had borrowed it from my aunt so I would have something nice to wear that day, since I only had old clothes. My cousin had good clothes. My aunt and cousin saw me stain the shirt.

Why do I remember this? Because it gave me the reputation of being a messy eater, something I was reminded about as late as age fifteen.

So, I have a sensitivity to ick. I'm sure this was also reinforced by the going-to-get-ice-cream-in-my-dad's-new-car incident. I'm not even sure which came first, the ice cream or the mustard. But, at some point when I was quite young, my dad got a new car. (This was the only car we had as a family but it was clearly Dad's Car.) My parents had a big fight about taking us kids out for ice cream cones. My dad didn't want us in the car. My mother insisted we could go out as a family, get ice cream, and have fun. Just like the neighbors.

It came down to my mom squatting in front of each of us, extracting individual promises that we would, in fact, eat ice cream cones without a single drip. She pretended to have a cone in her hand and demonstrated how we were to turn the cone and lick the bottom edge of the ice cream to make sure nothing dropped. And we promised. Once we got the cones, we got another round of individual lessons. And then we got in the back seat of the car with our ice cream cones. This was before the days of seat belts, so we freely bounced and squirmed and giggled as we ate our ice cream. And then someone let a drip drop. I'm not even sure if it was me. The scene ends with me frozen in place with fear, my stomach clenching.

The ice cream and mustard were icky, and therefore dangerous. Ick has become a generalized anxiety for me. It pops up at most meals in my present life with my present family. At some point, someone inevitably drips something or drags a sleeve over a serving dish or gets a dab of barbecue sauce on their finger. And my entire world shrinks to that misplaced spot. My heart pounds, my stomach clenches, and I jump and spurt "Watch out!" with the intensity of a scream condensed to the upper volume of a whisper.

My current family now refers to this as my "ick factor" and they attempt to compare one ick reaction to another using their self-designed ick-o-meter. But they also grab napkins and swipe the spots away as they gently tease — and reassure — me.

So ick is a quirk for me. It's just one of those things that distracts me and sets me on edge. No amount of rational understanding changes that. It's a scary moment in a horror film and my family reminds me that it's just a movie and we can move on.

Red splatters are something else. Spaghetti sauce or ketchup plops can leave me frozen, unable to breathe. If splattered across the floor, they can turn me into a clenched quivering sobbing huddle, muttering "I'm sorry, I'm sorry, I'm sorry, I'm sorry" before I even realize what dropped. It's a full-fledged flashback.

So, where the hell does this come from? What makes tomato different than mustard?

This is an example of ultimately remembering a traumatic incident only because I kept a clear memory of a reaction to the incident.

When I was small, my mother used to make a dish of stewed tomatoes baked in a piecrust. I clearly remember her assembling it one time when I was four or five. I saw it and panicked. My stomach hurt. I sobbed and begged her, "Please Mama, please Mama, don't make that Mama, I don't like that. Pleeeeeeeeeeaaaaaase" I grabbed hold of her right leg and cried. I was hysterical.

She stiffened but didn't look down from the counter. She shook her leg to loosen me and said, "Well, if you don't like it, you don't have to have any of it."

I was baffled.

And unconvinced.

"Really? Promise?"

"If you don't want any, it just means there is more for the rest of us." She shook me loose from her leg and refused to look at me. I felt a flood of relief and rejection.

My mother kept her promise and I didn't have to eat any of the stuff that evening. And she never made it again.

After my father's death many years later, the incident leading up to that scene came back to me.

It had essentially been a power struggle between my dad and me. Somewhere around age four or five, I had tried but didn't like the stewed tomato dish. He admonished me for rejecting something my mother had cooked — and he didn't let me have any other food until I finished it. I don't know how long I held out. I do remember the rest of my dinner being removed from my plate and I remember having the glass pie dish with the leftover gunk placed in front of me in the morning when everyone else was having cereal. I think it was also served for lunch. Whenever it was put in front of me, my siblings giggled. The older it got, the worse it looked. It dried out and sank toward the center of the dish, leaving a rubbery red edge stuck to the piecrust. The seeds became more obvious as they dried on the surface.

Of course, I gave in from hunger at some point, but it wasn't at a family meal. My father and I were at the table alone. There was nothing on the table but the pie plate of tomato leftovers, a fork and a napkin. I was sobbing. He said something like "I bet that should taste pretty good to you by now."

And I choked some of it down between my sobs. And then I threw up on the floor to the left of my chair.

And my dad said, "Don't you dare think that's going to get you out of this." No, he didn't make me eat my vomit but I'll tell you, the stewed tomato leftovers on the table looked about the same as the ones on the floor.

❧   ❧   ❧

Other triggers are not so specific and don't generate such specific responses. My anxiety just goes up. I startle more easily or in more places. Life and my reactions to it seem to become random. They're not, of course. But tracing a reaction to its original stimulus is rarely a straight shot, and finding the spark that lit that particular fire doesn't necessarily mean I can extinguish the blaze.

Life situations that seem to mirror my family dynamics can put me on high alert. Power plays, attempts at dominance, scapegoating and collusion mixed with gossip on the current side of my life screen can cause a themed montage on the past side to overwhelm my ability to cope with my present. To me, it becomes the tension before the storm in the cycle of abuse. Sometimes it is just that. Other times, it looks close enough. If I can recognize the connection, it helps. I can see the choices I have. Sometimes awareness changes my perspective. Sometimes awareness isn't enough and I just need to remove myself from the triggers.

Learning to live with PTSD has meant desensitizing myself as much as possible to triggers and avoiding those that I can't manage. (Yet.)

I feel ashamed of being vulnerable to triggers, to items and situations that others manage without much thought. It makes me feel like a wimp and, as I've said, I've spent much of my life trying to prove to myself that I'm not a wimp.

Memories

By definition, PTSD is focused on the past so memory, or lack thereof, is key. Many people with PTSD have gaps in their memories. That lack of continuity adds to the sense of life's randomness. And memories, their validity and the timing of their arousal, are one of the most controversial aspects of PTSD related to childhood trauma.

One factor that increases the likelihood of someone developing PTSD after a traumatic event is whether the event was deliberate, that is, whether the pain was inflicted intentionally by another human being. Since intentionally inflicting pain is usually illegal, memories of it are potentially incriminating evidence.

That can make reconstructing the past particularly hard for victims of child abuse.

Even if the victim never intends to file charges, putting the pieces together builds a case. That lifts the bar for accuracy: One has to be much more sure of traumatic memories than of, say, remembering the Halloween costume you wore when you were eight and, more specifically, the weather that night and if you had to wear your coat over your costume, which ruined it anyway.

It places those memories at the police station, in the center of an interrogation room lit by a single light bulb.

"Where were you on the night of August 14th the year you were five?"

And, if something was so traumatic that it messed you up, then, damn, you would think you would never forget it, right? So, what's with all this uncomfortable fuzziness?

The body's stress response during a traumatic event can affect how the brain stores memories of it. Memories of child abuse can be lost forever. If recalled in adulthood, they are referred to as recovered memories and they have been used as legal testimony in trials against perpetrators. Sometimes successfully, sometimes not.

Recovered memories. I hate the term. Perhaps it's because of the legal controversy that surrounds it, but more likely it just doesn't fit my image. To me, a recovered memory is an uncovered memory. It's a self-portrait that is suddenly revealed at an art opening as the veil is snapped away. It's observed as a whole, then appreciated in its parts. But always, it is a stand-alone visual piece.

My definition of memory has changed and expanded since I've accepted that I have PTSD and have slowly filled some of the gaps in my memory. I have more memories, but they are not additional individual self-portraits.

❧ ❧ ❧

It's a lot more complicated than that.

I had always thought of memories as something like stacks of chronologically ordered postcards, two-dimensional visual records of the past. Some cards were somewhat bigger than others, so they were always easy to find in the stack. A wedding day. The birth of a child. You could tell someone the story of what was on those cards without even having to look.

But most cards were the same size and not worth noting. Some were so similar that they were clumped together in theme piles: "I spent Saturday mornings eating cereal out of the box while watching cartoons on TV."

But most of the time, you don't think of them and couldn't recall any specific card on demand. (Um, where *was* I on the night of August 14th the year I was five?)

They're sort of like a collection of Christmas decorations. If you have one you value, each ornament has a story. However if you were asked, on any given day in July, to provide a complete inventory of your collection, from memory, odds are you couldn't do it. Yet, as you decorate your tree each year and gently unwrap each ornament, memories surface, the individual postcards come into view and you can tell the story. "Oh, look at these little guys! Connor made these elves for us when he was, what? Six? He just graduated from high school! Oh, and look at the one we got when we were in Hawaii! That was such a nice trip."

So there are piles of postcards that could tell countless stories. And there are stray postcards that don't quite fit. "This one? Well, that would have been before we moved to the new house, but I can't say when."

But mostly the piles just sit there while you live your life creating new postcards. And, in fact, many piles have to be put aside in order to live life. There are many World War II veterans who came home from war, went to work, raised families and never talked about their experiences. Retirement seems to have been a turning point for many. Once the daily structure of life was gone, the piles of postcards tumbled and many found themselves reliving the war through PTSD.

❡ ❡ ❡

I no longer think of my memories as simply two-dimensional postcards. They also have depth. Yes, memory includes sights, but there are also the smells and sensations and emotional tenor of a moment. These are the strands of experience that give memories their depth. And can bring them to life.

But these strands of deeper experience aren't necessarily stored with each mental image of the past, each postcard. They are stored separately, by strand, deep in the stacks of the library of my mind and body. The postcards? They're just the reference index cards.

Ideally, all strands of a remembered experience would be cross-referenced and, of course, linked to the index card: The smell of pumpkin pie links you to fun Thanksgivings at your beloved grandmother's and so, for a moment, as you walk by a kiosk in the mall that sells pumpkin pie-scented candles, you're flooded with warm feelings, a glimpse of your family and maybe a bit of hunger. You might even buy a candle. The marketers certainly hope so.

One of my earliest memories is of tottering along the side of our kitchen table, hands over my head, grasping the tabletop. My mother was sitting at the end, drinking coffee and having a cigarette. This was a familiar scene for me. I could see my mom's hands move in and out of sight, from the table to her face as she lifted her cup, her cigarette, or some other item, but I never knew what she was getting until her hands moved into sight again. I would pull myself up but could never see what was on the table. Until the day that I could! This is still one of the most delightful memories of my life. I could see what was on the table! The whole world was open to me!

So, the postcard is the plane of the tabletop coming into view. It links me to a feeling of complete wonder and joy of discovery, which is shelved in the stacks and clearly cross-referenced with the table viewing. It would make sense to me that it would also link me to the smell of coffee and cigarette smoke, but it doesn't. Perhaps that was too common to identify.

But this cross-referenced system linking the postcard to the various strands of remembered experience isn't perfect. There are memory strands that may be linked, such as the smell of burning leaves and a gagging sensation, which are disconnected from the postcard that might tell its story. Since it makes no logical sense, it is just another mystery reaction to the world. The scary-boxes-in-the-hallway quirk.

The memory strands that are associated with splatters have, for the most part, been reconnected with the reference postcards that explain their story. That doesn't alleviate my reactions to them, but it does help explain them, which makes me feel less crazy.

❧ ❧ ❧

Sometimes the postcard is retrieved from a single strand of memory. An older sibling once referred to a time when we stayed at our aunt's for a couple of weeks when our mother was hospitalized and the youngest was an infant. I didn't know what she was talking about. She said, "Don't you remember, we slept up in the attic bedroom under the eaves?" And suddenly I remembered it all. I was seven. There was a tiny window at the head of the bed and everything smelled sort of funny. I had to share a bed with my younger sister. I was already sensitized to the terrors of the night, so I couldn't stand having her touch me. The baby screamed and screamed. And I missed my mom. I really loved my aunt and uncle but I ached for my mom. And my own bed.

It was all there. The two of us sitting at the top of the stairs. My aunt making me fried corn pone, which I had never had before. Lying on her bed with the baby. They had a chenille bedspread with a big circular pattern in the middle that I traced with my finger and then smoothed as if I were petting a cat.

It was all there, brought to me by the strand of memory about sleeping under an eave. But a single strand can also lead you astray, if you mistake it for the postcard.

🍂 🍂 🍂

I played the flute for a year when I was in sixth grade. My older sister played the clarinet at the same age. Or so I thought. Years later, she would tell me that she never played the clarinet and I would insist on having seen her hold it while standing next to the kitchen table. She finally argued, "Don't you think I would remember if I played an instrument? Don't you think I would remember practicing or playing in the band?" And I had to admit that, yes, she would remember that. So, where did this image of my big sister with a clarinet come from?

The rest of the memory came back with a smack. She had been holding the clarinet, crying. My father was screaming at my mother that there was no way in hell he was spending money to rent an instrument and he didn't care if my sister's class schedule was all set.

I have no idea why, a few years later, I was allowed to play flute. Neither does my sister.

My sister had chosen the clarinet. Chosen, not played. I had chosen the flute. The strand I clung to was of a shared interest and bonding between my sister and me. I had wished that sliver of unity into a story in which we each played our chosen instrument. And that had become my reality.

🍃 🍃 🍃

There are also emotional strands of memory that are in a category of their own. They're the ones associated with secrets. They are replicated and passed from one generation to the next almost unnoticed. They are the accumulation of small cues, tension in the room when a name is mentioned or a quick change of subjects. A simple question that is answered after a pause that is just a bit too long. The recipient never gets the full story, the postcard, just the ripple of the charge that hangs in the room. These often get braided together into a story that makes some sort of sense, although that narrative may lie just below our awareness, until something happens and it surfaces as an obvious "fact."

"Damn, Great Uncle Joe was gay, wasn't he?"

"Damn, Mom got an abortion as a teenager, didn't she?"

These revelations come together as BFOs (Blinding Flashes of the Obvious). Well, duh? You just KNOW the truth, although there may be no way to prove it. All the players may be dead (although there may still be an elderly relative who winks at you when you finally ask the right question). The "facts" didn't occur in your lifetime, yet you feel the effects. Your family felt like men should be married by age

30 or it was somehow . . . unseemly. The "stay a virgin until you're married" message to girls was a little too . . . hysterical. We learned as much by what was not said as by what was said.

❧   ❧   ❧

There was an unspoken emotional strand that ran through my father's family for two generations before at least three great-grandchildren independently reached similar conclusions and tentatively tested them against each other's perceptions.

The "truth" we reached is that our great-grandfather, a wealthy, overbearing man who deliberately controlled key aspects of his children's lives well into adulthood, was somehow instrumental in the suicide by carbon monoxide poisoning of our grandfather, the socially acceptable but violent drunk who had married his daughter. We have awkwardly sketched a postcard to reference that strand that each of us feels.

But we don't all interpret it the same way.

To me, it was also a lesson to the next generation about the costs of breaking the patriarch's rules. He sent two of his teenage grandsons, my father and his cousin (who was not a blood relative of my grandfather), to the north woods of Michigan to identify the body.

My deceased grandfather had brothers and other adult family members who could have handled this. But my great-grandfather directed his son-in-law's death arrangements and specifically identified who should take on this grisly

task: two young grandsons who were on the verge of stepping out of his sphere of control.

The message I took from that? Step out of line and the
head of the family can kill you. Is it true? Who knows? It's
certainly not provable in a court of law. But is it reality?

For me, yes, it is, based partly on my father's frequent
rages against us when he thought we were being too independent or didn't respect him enough. The proof of that reality, however, was the look in my father's eyes as he choked
me. He was angry, but he wasn't out of control with anger
or alcohol. He was coolly deciding whether to exercise his
God-given right to kill me, to control his family. Just as his
grandfather had.

And I knew I was at his mercy.

❧   ❧   ❧

Memories, facts, reality. They're all supposed to be the
same, aren't they? And everyone should agree on them, right?

I know that I have holes in my memory and suspect that
I have reached incorrect conclusions about those that are
intact, but I have no idea which those might be. Still, it's
what I have and I've settled into having a "working reality."
That is, I know what is true for me but I am open to hearing
others' reality. I may incorporate some of their reality into
mine, or I may just accept that there are differences.

Presence and Absence

I know that I was sexually abused as a young child not so much because I remember moments of clear violation. No, what I remember are the times I got yelled at for doing the things that are now clearly identified as markers of childhood sexual abuse: inappropriate sexual behavior, repetitive play that reenacts the abuse, and difficulty sleeping.

This was terribly confusing to me. When I was four or five, Grandpa D., my mom's foster dad, liked playing doctor and horsey with my sisters and me. He would play with us in the living room on the couch with the scratchy gold upholstery while Mom stayed in the kitchen. This is the man who had impregnated my mom as a teenager, taken her to New York for an abortion and then given her a diamond ring as a consolation gift. She couldn't have been blind to his interest in her children, but she stayed in the kitchen.

So playing horsey was okay with Grandpa D. It fact, it was expected. And, when I tried to play horsey with an uncle during a family picnic, everyone laughed. At first. But I kept doing it. I was slapped, yelled at and dragged away. I was embarrassed but didn't really know why. It was just more evidence that anything weird could happen at any time. Nothing was predictable, but I was supposed to know when and why these shifts happened.

And then there were the times that I would play quietly by myself with my Barbie. My Barbie had a very hard life. She was usually held captive and sexually humiliated. Sometimes my mom would see me and scream, "Can't you think of any other games to play with your doll?" I didn't know what she meant or why she was mad. I was just playing with my Barbie.

❡ ❡ ❡

Sleep. Sleep has always been an issue for me. I don't know when it started but I suspect it was when I was very young and in the hospital. I had four eye surgeries and my tonsils out before I was five. I was also hospitalized several times for pneumonia. My earliest memory is of standing in a crib in a hospital, not quite able to look over the top of the bars.

Parents were only allowed to visit once a day and the nurses were a lot nicer to you when your parents were there. Once, my mom brought me some little pop bottles made of wax. I bit off the top to drink the sweet syrup inside but I dribbled it on the sheet. It was brown and those little drops quickly spread to blotches. I started to cry, but my mom said it was okay. She got the nurse who said not to worry; she would take care of it.

When my mom left, the nurse came in and spanked me for making her change the sheets.

My father rarely visited me in the hospital but, when he did, it was a very big deal. He showed up one afternoon and told me that my mom couldn't come, so he came and he said he would come see me the next day, too. He didn't stay long, but promised that he would not only see me the next day but he would bring me a sucker.

I was excited. I told every nurse I saw that my daddy was coming to see me and he was bringing me a sucker.

My crib was in a nook near a window directly across from the door to the room. Between the door and my bed were other kids in other beds with curtains pulled around them.

I saw my dad enter the room because it was a straight shot from my bed to the door. He walked in and I jumped up. "Daddy, Daddy." He came up to me, lifted me from the crib and held me tight. I hugged him and asked, "Did you bring me my sucker?"

He dropped me cold. "That's all you really care about isn't it?" he asked, and then he turned and walked out.

I ached. I cried. When the nurses asked if my daddy had come to see me yet, I was ashamed, but I didn't really know why.

The night nurses never saw your parents so they never had to pretend to like you. They got especially mad if they came in at night and you were awake. But there were also other people, maybe the orderlies, who did like little kids and they would sneak in at night to "check you out" if you weren't awake enough to possibly make noise.

So, at night, every adult wanted you unconscious. For some, it was dangerous if you were not; for others, it was dangerous if you were. The hall lights were never turned off at night and the room door was always left half-open. You could see the outline of someone walking into the room but could never tell who it was until they were near the bed.

I learned not to sleep, not because I was afraid of sleep or nightmares. I learned not to sleep because I was afraid of what I would wake up to. If it wasn't a lone figure handling my body in the dark, it was a group of people under stark lights, lifting me onto a gurney that would take me to the room where four of them held me down while a fifth forced a mask over my face so that all I could breathe was that awful, awful air.

It was ether, of course, the anesthetic of the day. After inhaling, I would see squiggly lines that looked sort of like the clothes hanging in the closet when I would sneak in there, lie on the floor and look up.

I would wake up later, still smelling ether and vomiting. Half of my head would be bandaged. But my mom was usually there.

❧ ❧ ❧

My not sleeping became a very big issue at home. I can remember toddling out of bed long after my siblings went to sleep because I was so bored. If my mom were still up, she would shoo me back to bed. When I complained that I couldn't sleep, she told me to think about nothing.

I spent a lot of hours lying in bed trying to think about nothing. As a four-year-old, my made-up meditation technique was to envision a big white sheet and then think about what was on it, which was, of course, nothing. But my mind always wandered back to the sheet itself or how it was hung up. And then I would try to think of nothing again.

If I ventured out of bed after my dad got home (he was always "working late," meaning at the bar, and we rarely saw him before bed), he would explode at both my mom and me. He was mad at me for not obeying and at my mom for not being able to control me.

I think that's when my mom started giving me Benadryl at night. It was still a prescription drug then so she must have gotten it from a doctor or pharmacist. I assume it was children's strength. I just remember the routine we developed. She would lift me up to sit on the kitchen counter, and then reach behind a cookbook on a nearby shelf to retrieve the silver packet of pills. She would tear open a section of the packet to reveal a flat yellow disc that she would give me. It looked sort of like a Necco wafer with a line down the middle of it and tasted a little like lemon.

And then I would sleep, but I would have problems sleeping most nights for the rest of my life.

And, to this day, if someone walks into a room where I am sleeping, I am likely to startle, jerking, gasping, sometimes yelling, although I may not wake up.

Or so I am told.

Breaking

I broke in sixth grade. That I know.

I got stuck at an early age but, as far as PTSD is concerned, I broke in sixth grade. Being stuck meant I would freeze. Time would stop. Breaking meant that the past would also flood the present. Life lost any sense of continuity.

My early childhood was rough. There were abuse and traumatic medical procedures. My mom disappeared at times and, at others, I would find her just lying on the floor breathing into a paper bag (a technique that I later learned was a method of dealing with the hyperventilation that comes with panic attacks).

My dad was generally not around. When he was, he was alternately embracing and terrifying; sometimes he was both at the same time. When I was eight, he and I would sit out on the front stoop at night in the summer (since I wasn't sleeping anyway). Once he flicked his cigarette butt onto the asphalt drive and told me to go put it out with my foot. I was barefoot. I hesitated but he kept encouraging me, "Go on, you can do it." Eventually, I thought maybe I could and I knew that, if I did, he would be so proud of me and my toughness. It took awhile for me to get up my nerve, but I walked over and stepped on the ember.

And immediately jumped off. It hurt like hell.

He laughed and laughed at me because I was so stupid that I would do such a thing.

❡   ❡   ❡

So, I got stuck pretty early. Demanding situations would leave me immobilized and confused. By third grade, I was the kid who would freeze in the outfield while playing softball. Because of my vision problems, I have no depth perception. Balls seemed to move at random. The sudden expectation of action overwhelmed me. I got hit in the face with balls on occasion but that wasn't nearly as painful as having kids be mad at me for my incompetence. I had perceived danger and froze. I may or may not have been injured, but in either case, I had pissed everyone off. I got disoriented and scared and then I would cry. That, of course, just made me so much more attractive to the athletes selecting their teams. When I was the last kid standing, teachers kindly gave me the role of keeping score. At least I was good at math.

❡   ❡   ❡

But, in sixth grade, a jumble of experiences left me numb, miserable and desperate. I couldn't keep my postcards connected to their strands of memory. I lost postcards. I started living life on the split-screen television; only it was different than it is now. Instead of my current life on one side and the montage of clips from my past on the other, I had my current life on one side and a gaping, three-dimensional hole on the other. If I was doing well in the present the hole would shrink, but it could widen and swallow me at any moment.

At the time, I saw all of this as centering on my mom's mental illness. She cried more. She hallucinated more. She was hospitalized more. I missed her. I ached for her when she was gone. We were not yet old enough to visit her in the psych ward so we just waited for her to come home.

At first my dad tried to run the household. He came home after work rather than going to the bars. He would try to cook meals and would give us jobs to do around the house. It felt strange, though, and intrusive. He was not a part of our daily lives because our schedules had never fit. He was an appendage to our family and a potentially explosive one at that.

He had higher standards of cleanliness than my mother and we never met them. One of my clearest memories of not doing a good enough job is another memory-once-removed. I don't remember the action, but I remember leaving the house and walking for hours in a rage, replaying the scene in my head. I had washed the kitchen floor. He told me to prove that I thought I had done a good enough job, pushed me to the floor, held my face down, and told me to lick it. He wouldn't let me up until I did.

It was during that long, fuming walk that I first started to think about how I could repay my father for any money he had ever spent on me. I wanted to buy my freedom.

❡ ❡ ❡

When my mom was gone, we usually came home from school to an empty house. But, one afternoon, our dad and aunt were both there, waiting for us. My dad stopped us at the front door, told us that Mom was home only for a visit but we had to be quiet and nice to her.

She was in the living room, sitting on the edge of the davenport, as if formally posed with her legs to the side, ankles crossed, hands clasped in her lap.

We ran in and yelled "Hi Mama!" It was so good to see her. I had missed her so much. She looked up at us and started to sob. But she hadn't seen me. She hadn't seen any of us. She looked past us. She was different.

My dad screamed that we were too loud and sent us to our rooms. My mother was quickly taken back to the hospital and my aunt made us dinner. None of us mentioned Mom or Dad.

I identify that as the turning point, although I can't say that for sure. My postcards for this patch of my history have been shuffled and reshuffled many times, but they still don't make a clear story line. At this point I just assume that some postcards are missing, although I still have their brash painful strands of memory.

Our daily life changed. My dad never came home early in the evening after that. Sometimes he would come in around 9 or 10 p.m. with groceries, but mostly we were on our own for meals, doing laundry and getting off to school. Sometimes our neighbors would bring casseroles over for us, which was always a nice surprise. How did they know we weren't very organized with meals?

My mother came home from the hospital a couple of weeks later. She didn't sob. She didn't hug us. She was flat. I found out later that this was when she had her first series of electroshock therapy, circa 1966. She was never the same. Neither were our lives.

❧ ❧ ❧

When she was back home, she made efforts to assert her Mom-ness, but we simply humored her. At one point, she told me that I couldn't ride my bike along a certain street because it was too dangerous. I stared at her and wanted to scream, "Who the hell do you think you are to tell me what I can and can't do? You've been locked away. I could ride anywhere last week and no one would know or care." But when I looked at her, I couldn't say a thing. She was obviously more in need of care than able to provide it. I said that was fine, I would just stay with her at the house. I was about eleven.

She would wake early, smoke cigarettes and drink coffee before she got us up for school. She said that was her personal time of the day and she liked the quietness of the house before we got up. She made us Malt-O-Meal for breakfast. (My father wouldn't allow oatmeal in the house, because it looked too much like vomit, in the same way he wouldn't allow rice in the house, because it looked too much like maggots.)

The Malt-o-Meal was always cold by the time she woke us. So, our groggy, dark mid-winter Michigan mornings started with a clump of congealed Malt-O-Meal surrounded by a moat of milk. Once I hit that part of my geography studies, I always called it the Rock of Gibraltar. Put enough sugar on it and it was fine. Put enough sugar on anything and it will seem fine.

We went to school and would come home to Mom sleeping on the loveseat in the den, the knitted green afghan tucked around her boney self, her unfiltered cigarettes, lighter and ashtray within reach. We would gently wake her and she would radiantly smile when she saw us. She would ask about our days. And then, more often than not, she would declare it a "Fix It Your Own" evening, like it was a special event. Fix It Your Own meant we were to fend for ourselves for dinner. I would usually eat cold cereal. Sometimes one of my siblings would make something out of whatever canned goods we had and our selection of salt, pepper, oregano, basil and Lawry's Seasoned Salt. They would feed the youngest, since cold cereal for dinner wasn't very popular. If it looked like there might be some of the concoction left over, I would ask for it but I wasn't interested in cooking.

Then we cleaned up the kitchen. Sometimes our mom would watch television with us, but usually she just took her pills and went to bed early. She would shuffle down the hall to her bedroom, her ankle joints clicking as she walked.

And the house transitioned. We were back on our own. We did our homework or talked with friends on the phone or watched television and did whatever else needed to be done.

About once a week, my father would come home before we kids had all gone to bed.

◊ ◊ ◊

My father had his own routine, his own schedule. He worked retail, which meant he didn't have to go to work until mid-morning and he worked into the evenings. It also meant that he never got a full weekend off. His days off were Sunday and Tuesday.

I hated Sundays, but Tuesdays were fine as long as the weather was good. He was a golfer and would be out on the course (and at the clubhouse bar) all day. But you never knew for sure. I remember walking home from the school bus stop one day, turning the corner that brought our house into sight and seeing his car in the driveway. My stomach clenched. I told my mom this and her response was, "I know, Honey, I feel the same way."

My father even ate different food than we did. He had his own shelf of canned mushrooms, asparagus and potatoes that we weren't allowed to touch. When my mom bought and cooked items to be shared among the whole family, the division was clear. If she bought a cantaloupe, my father got half and the rest was split among the rest of us. If we roasted chicken on the grill on a Sunday, we roasted two. My father got one and the rest of us shared the second. Cottage cheese was only for him. It cost too much for us. He kept his personal supply of orange juice in the refrigerator.

If we asked nicely, sometimes he would give us a taste.

But the most notable difference in our diets had to do with steak. My father loved steak and saw having it as a sign that he had made it in the world. He would come home long after Mom had gone to bed and we kids had had another Fix It Your Own dinner, often carrying a grocery bag with the steak and other special items he would have for dinner himself. If he were home early enough that we kids were still up and he was in a good mood, he would cook and let us watch. He would explain every step he took as if it were a cooking lesson. He would sauté mushrooms and onions in a pan with butter, while heating his steak plate in the oven. Then he would fry his steak and place it on the steak plate so that it sizzled, and drip the fried mushrooms and onions over it.

He was very proud of his steak plate. It was a metal oval with drip channels that was set in a wooden holder for serving. It was the kind of plate used in restaurants ("Watch out, that plate is hot!") and he had one.

We kids would hang around. If he thought we were good and he was feeling benevolent, he might give us a bite. He would cut it, stab it with a fork and offer it to us as if it were communion at a Catholic Mass.

We kids were hungry. For food. For attention. For love. To feel special to someone. My father created much of that hunger, then generously eased it a bit through tiny pieces of meat. One of my siblings remembers getting those single bites and sucking on them until they dissolved.

We appreciated it. We *had* to appreciate it. I once casually said I wasn't hungry and didn't want a taste. It enraged him. Who the hell did I think I was that I would reject a piece of steak? How could I be so independent and ungrateful? My siblings tensed up. I took the piece of steak and answered, "Yes," when he asked, "Now, isn't that delicious?" He laughed and wondered why I would be so silly as to pass that up.

He decided if he would give us something on any particular night. He also decided that we would accept it when offered. Period. There were nights when we got the youngest out of bed so that everyone got a bite.

As an aside, while cleaning out my dad's apartment after his death, my siblings and I found one of his steak plates. I immediately wanted it. A sib grimaced and said, "Why in the hell would you want that thing?" I thought for a moment and said, "It proves it was real."

On the nights that my dad did not come home by ten or so, we all just drifted to our own endings of the day. Eventually the lights went out, much as they do between stage settings in a play.

But, just as on a stage, much was going on when it looked dark and quiet.

I couldn't sleep. I shared a bedroom with a younger sister at the time and I would make up stories to tell her in the dark. The only one I can remember had to do with smuggling diamonds by embedding them in the corks of wine bottles. She would tell me when she was ready to go to sleep and I would shut up.

Sometimes I drifted off; sometimes I tried to think of nothing but blank white sheets. But I was always awake at 2:30 a.m. That's when the bars closed. That's when I expected my dad to come home. And every night, sometime between 2:45 and 3:15 a.m., his car would pull into the driveway, the headlights shooting through our bedroom window and sweeping across the wall, changing size as he neared the curve to the garage, then snapping out of sight as the garage door opener would crank into gear.

Act Two had begun at our house.

❧ ❧ ❧

I usually got up to see my dad when he came home. It may have started just because I was awake, but my dad was usually in a pretty good mood at that time of night and wanted to talk.

My father had always told me that he could talk to me when he couldn't talk to anyone else. He said I was special that way because I had been born on his birthday. He made it sound like we were in a secret club.

I loved the attention, so our late-night talks became a routine. I don't ever remember telling him anything about school or my life. He just talked, sometimes about work (he hated his bosses) and sometimes about people he spent time with at the bar. But, mostly he talked to me about his problems. He complained about my mom. He complained about how he didn't have as much money as he should because my mother's medical bills were so high. He complained about my siblings.

He would also tell me how someone at the bar had suggested that he just beat the crap out of my mom and that would set her straight, or that a sibling deserved a good beating. He would ask me what I thought and it became my job to talk him out of it. He loved watching me work to convince him.

I took that responsibility seriously. As much as I appreciated the attention I got, I was also trying to monitor him. I had a better relationship with him than others in the family and I felt it was up to me to try to soften his impact. I would warn my sibs when something in particular seemed to bother him.

I would also tell my mother when he had done something to make her feel crazier. For example, at one time my mother was delusional and believed that there were people living in our attic who would come down at night and use the kitchen. Before going to bed, she would carefully mark chairs with chalk and place string between cabinet door handles so that, in the morning, she could check for evidence of their presence. One of the things my dad would do when he came home at night was look for any of these markers and alter them. He smeared chalk, moved string and laughed.

The next morning, I would get up as early as my mother to explain what had happened. I would make her sit down, look her in the eye, forget everything around me and try to speak from the most calm, honest part of me I could find. I needed to be completely open and trustworthy with her if she was going to have any faith in the reality I was offering. It usually worked.

Then I would eat my Malt-O-Meal, get my homework together and go to school.

❧   ❧   ❧

I don't remember my father ever carrying through on any of the specific threats he had made during our talks, but he was getting more physically violent with my siblings. He had pushed me a lot but never hit me.

I guess this "special" relationship with my dad was hurtful to one of my siblings, who walked into the house with my dad one evening about nine. The three of us were in the kitchen, near the table.

I knew immediately that something was wrong but I had no idea what. My father wouldn't look at me. He set something on the table, looked down at it for a moment and then lunged at me. He slammed me against the wall and seethed, "You bitch."

I was utterly overwhelmed. I had no idea what he was pissed about.

"Dad?"

"Don't you dare fucking 'Dad' me, you bitch."

He grabbed me by the throat, lifted me and started slamming me against the wall. I had never seen him quite like this. In a rage but not completely out of control. Steeled. "You think you're so fucking smart don't you? Don't you? You think you're smarter than me, don't you? Well you're not, Goddamn it! And I'm going to hear you say it. Say it. Say I'm smarter than you. Say it, damn it!"

All the while he was choking and slamming me.

I assume I said it, but I don't know. I either passed out or otherwise went away. I was out of there.

When I came back, I was in a heap on the kitchen floor. There was a pair of shoes near my head. I looked up and saw my sibling who smiled and said, "Now you know what it feels like, bitch," and walked away.

I don't remember anything else about that night but sometime in the next week or so, I again ventured out to the kitchen to see my dad after he had been home for a while. It was the middle of the night. He was cooking a steak, I could smell it.

Our kitchen had a pocket door that he had closed. I slid it open, walked in and leaned against the wall near the refrigerator. He didn't look up from the frying pan, which

I knew was a bad sign but by now he had seen me, so I was committed.

"Hi."

"What do you want?"

"I just wanted to see how you were doing."

He continued to stare at the frying pan, then moved it to another burner and turned toward me. He took the three steps between us and pushed me against the wall with his whole body. I didn't know what was going on. He wasn't hurting me but he wasn't hugging me either. Then he started grabbing me and put his hands into my pajamas.

I know I got upset and I again passed out or went away. When I came back, I was on the floor and still had all my clothes on. He was at the stove again. He looked at me and said, "I don't know what you're so upset about. You're the one who's always getting up to see me."

And then he insisted on my having a bite of steak. And he watched me to make sure I chewed and swallowed it. Then I was allowed to get up and go back to bed.

Needless to say, I never got up to see him late at night again. But that didn't really solve the problem. I was terrified of him. And he continued to be terrifying. When my mother was hospitalized (which was more and more often), he began coming home after the bars closed, bursting into our rooms and pulling us out of bed. He would line us up and scream at us about how lazy we were, how the food we ate cost too much money and what an awful job we did of keeping up the house. Sometimes he would have us clean in the middle of the night.

♂   ♂   ♂

So this is when I broke. I was crawling out of my skin with anxiety.

Or I was numb. This is the year in which I was in the band and took flute lessons. I could not, for the life of me, figure out rhythm. I wasn't on the current side of my split-screen life. I was too numb. I had an incredibly hard time connecting one moment to the next, so following a pattern seemed impossible. I remember the band teacher setting up a metronome for me to use in class. I just stared at it in confusion. I was so numb or out of touch that I had no clue when the next click would be. It seemed totally random. And I felt great pressure to do this seemingly simple action. I have such a clear picture of watching the metronome and having it freeze mid-motion, although I am sure that it was me who froze.

This is also the year that I started to resent gym class. I was being forced to do things with my body that were not of my own choosing. Doing required jumping jacks didn't seem much different than the scene in those old Westerns in which the bad guy starts shooting at someone's feet, laughs and says, "Now dance!"

The following few years are a patchwork for me. I was there and I wasn't. When I was there I was on guard. My mother was there and she wasn't. I was captive in my father's house. Everyone was either in need or in danger of getting hurt. I was hungry sometimes. I had two outfits to wear to school, if you consider one gray skirt and two blouses to be two outfits. My knee socks were hand-me-downs from my cousin and had to be kept in place with rubber bands. My classmates went to dances, shopped with their moms on Saturdays, and discovered fashion.

I was talking my mother into coming back to the house when she went for midnight walks barefoot in the January snow, and talking my dad out of beating her up.

❧   ❧   ❧

There are many lasting effects of this stretch of time, although it took me decades to identify them.

One that I experience daily is the symptom of avoidance. It's very common for people with PTSD to avoid circumstances and settings that remind them of a traumatic event. People who have been in car accidents may find it hard to drive again.

I avoid food. I hate thinking about it. I wish I didn't have to bother with eating but not because I dislike food. I have favorite foods. I like being able to choose from a variety of prepared items, like at a deli counter or a big, relaxed, sit-down dinner.

But the whole concept of food is tainted by power for me. It's something that can be withheld or forced upon you. Decades ago, I found it hard to go into grocery store produce departments because the fruits and vegetables seemed to be arranged like soft porn. Enticing, but with a price.

Now, I'll buy fresh produce but I can't face it if it's not eaten within a couple of days. That slip away from the peak of freshness can make me feel almost ill. Unfortunately, since I don't like to think about food and don't make big plans for using it, I waste a lot of produce when I buy it for myself. So I generally don't.

Left to my own devices, I'll eat some form of cheese and carbohydrate when I'm hungry.

That said, I have to admit that I'm a bit of a food hoarder. Canned goods, pasta, things that won't rot.

So was my dad.

Going and Returning

A reaction to acute stress that appears to be a risk factor in developing chronic PTSD is dissociation or, as I've always thought of it, "going away." Dissociation happens when a part of you steps out of the current traumatic situation because, well, you just can't handle it. It's a version of the little kid's belief that "If I close my eyes, you can't see me." In this case, it's "If I close myself, you can't hurt me."

One form of dissociation is having an out-of-body experience, in which you float above the event that's occurring. At other times, it doesn't feel as if you've left your body but rather, that you've curled into a hard little ball that can't hear or feel anything.

And then there is the milder but longer lasting version of going away: emotional numbing.

One of the worst weeks of my life culminated in one of the worst nights of my life. I was twenty-three.

In a matter of three days, I had been informed that I might be developing a tumor in my eye, that my relationship was ending, and that I had not gotten a job I had applied for and really, really wanted. At the end of that third day, when I received the job rejection, I went home to my apartment, made myself a Black Russian, sipped it while I took a hot bath, and then got ready for bed. I put on a record (Gerry Rafferty, because I wanted to hear Baker Street), turned off the lights and got into bed.

Sometime before the album finished, there was a man standing over my bed in my darkened room holding a weapon over his head. It looked like a knife, but I couldn't tell for certain. He told me not to make a noise or he would hurt me. He did anyway. And he raped me.

But there was a time, a second, a moment, an hour, when he held me in front of him and I was certain I was about to have a knife slide between my ribs and I would be killed. Time stopped. I became so acutely aware of being alive that the air I breathed seemed to turn to something thicker, like water, ebbing and flowing from my lungs. Each moment might have been my last.

And then I went away. I just went away. I left my body and floated to the ceiling, up to the left corner above my bed, where I could watch myself below. I stayed there until I realized that, from some distance away, this person was talking to me. I thought, "I have to go back now, so I can hear what he is saying." He said he was leaving. I was to stay in the room and not move for half an hour and, if I called the police, he would be back.

I heard him leave through the front door (he had gotten in through a window). I waited a moment and, without turning on any lights, snuck into my kitchen, got a knife, and then called the police. I answered the door when the cruiser arrived, with my knife overhead, ready to strike.

I was treated at the hospital and released. Friends were there and supportive. I was moved out of my apartment so I never needed to return.

But I was a mess. This qualified as an acute stress reaction. It was hard to live from moment to moment. I couldn't focus enough to read. I had a hard time holding a conversation. When I tried to sleep, I kept knives within reach and moved furniture to block doorways.

❦ ❦ ❦

There are three pieces to this story I want you to understand. The first has to do with my out-of-body experience. The second has to do with my reaction to my hospital assessment and the third is, well, when I came back.

My dissociation the night I was raped was unnerving to me, even though I couldn't actually concentrate enough to think about it at the time. What hit me was how familiar it felt. I had gone away countless times before but had forgotten about it. Mostly, I had gone away from my dad.

The times that were easiest to recall were when he tickled me. When I was somewhere between three and six, my dad would jump on me from behind on the living room floor and start "tickling" me. I hated it. I was fighting his ever-moving hands and shrieking, begging him to stop. And then it would suddenly be over and I would be on the floor by myself. When I remembered these times, I always thought that he must have kept it up until I gagged and passed out, then I came to by myself. The night I was raped, I realized that I had gone away all those times, just as I had those two nights he attacked me in the kitchen.

I remembered knowing that I had that ability, though. In high school, when drugs were abundant, I remember thinking that I could go away on my own if I really needed to. I thought of it as "stepping back from my face."

Sometimes I did an imitation for my siblings of my mom as she was starting to lose it, which I now believe was a form of dissociating.

I would sit quietly in a chair, and say, "Okay, I'm going to do Mom now." I would stare ahead and go away just a bit, step back from my face just a bit. I would settle back away and my eyes would lose focus.

Once when I did this, one of my siblings got upset and screamed, "Stop it! Stop it! I hate it when you do that!"

To me, the trick made my mom's disappearances more understandable and was something I could joke about with the sliver of the world that would appreciate it. I realized it wasn't appreciated and I never did it as entertainment again.

ø ø ø

I went to the hospital after I was raped. A friend met me there. The nurses were very nice, if confused, about what to do. Physically, I was mostly intact and they knew what to do with the parts that were not. However, the state had just instituted a standard sexual assault evidence-collection kit and no one had ever used one before. I got to listen as one nurse slowly read the instructions to everyone else. I was poked, samples were taken, and one kind nurse kept patting my arm and saying, "I'm sorry, Honey."

I left the hospital with two gifts. The first was the effects of a single dose of Valium. I had never had a benzodiazepine before and I clearly remember it hitting my system. I was in a wheelchair waiting to go out to the car. Suddenly, I could form sentences again. I could ask questions. I could read the paperwork that the medical staff and police had given me. I read the medical assessment and stopped at the section labeled "Patient reaction." Someone had handwritten "Normal/Appropriate" in the blank provided.

That was the second gift.

I had been totally unable to monitor or evaluate my feelings or actions in that situation. I was completely lost. I had had to scrape my consciousness off the bedroom ceiling two hours before. I kept checking to see if my body was intact.

Yet this was seen as "Normal/Appropriate." I felt crazy, but I wasn't crazy. Not according to these people, anyway. Not under these circumstances. That was incredibly reassuring but didn't give me a clue as to what to do next, what was appropriate next.

I still have that paperwork; it was so precious to me. As awful as it was, I was officially okay at the time.

I got a week off work to heal and move. People would comment on how hard it might be for a while. My emotional and verbal responses were, "Not me." I had dealt with enough shit. This was just another layer and it pissed me off. This wasn't even from my family. This was in the larger world, which had always felt safer to me, where I was doing everything I was supposed to be doing, and "Wham!" I was back to being vulnerable and humiliated.

I kept the postcard, the story, but crammed all the sensory strands of that memory as far away as I could. I didn't order them, shelve them, or cross-reference them. They were pushed away and closed up.

That helped me function to some degree, although for many months I would completely lose my ability to concentrate at times. Once I regained some level of equilibrium and was able to work again (sort of) I had to think of what to do next with my life. I already had PTSD (although I didn't know it), which meant my sense of the future was foreshortened. My job was horrible and was made worse after the rape. At organizational functions that served alcohol, the executive director would get drunk, corner me, and then "sympathetically" ask for details about the rape.

It was 1978. Sexual harassment in the workplace wasn't talked about. I was having a hard enough time pushing the police to investigate the assault. (Although a suspect was identified, and believed to have been stalking me for at least a couple of weeks, no charges were ever filed. I found out a year after I was raped that this suspect was related to the chief of police by marriage. I got this news from a friend in the prosecutor's office the same day that my personal belongings — sheets with squares of cloth snipped out of them — were returned to me from the state crime lab.)

I wasn't fighting another battle. All I wanted was out. I wanted to get on with my life, although I wasn't quite sure what that meant. I didn't have goals as much as visions of escape.

❧ ❧ ❧

I did get away. I went overseas. And I discovered that there is no such thing as a geographical cure. I dragged my neatly wrapped box of shit with me.

But the box wasn't actually full of shit. It was full of the strands of memory that I just couldn't sort and reference and *feel*. They were from my early childhood and from my recent rape. They were a black hole of grief and fear. If I opened the box, they would engulf and incapacitate me, and turn me into that quivering puddle that I knew was the real me.

That pretty handmade paper that covered the box? That is the numbing that comes with PTSD, the layer that separates me from my scary stuff. It's the layer that allowed me to move through life without quite living it. It was as neat and tidy as I could get it. It allowed me to function as I thought people were supposed to function.

But numbing also makes life flat. Flat is better than hellish, of course, but it does get boring. This can lead people with PTSD to seek some sort of extra stimulation in order to feel alive. Sometimes that comes in the form of hurtful practices like cutting. It can lead to soldiers requesting another deployment, so that at least their hypervigilance has a purpose. But it can also take the shape of thrill-seeking behavior. This creates the paradox that, while feeling extreme fear internally, you take risks that others consider quite brave.

Of course, if you don't believe you have a tomorrow, there isn't much to lose.

Being hypervigilant and numb at the same time may seem like a contradiction, but it's not. Both lock you into this very precise moment. The past is flat and gone. The next second may be horrifying. You are here and now, and very, very wary.

❧ ❧ ❧

Three years and two ocean crossings after I was raped as an adult, it hit me again. Either my numbing handmade paper had worn thin or there was a direct puncture. It doesn't matter, the box opened and I was yanked back to the night I was raped.

I was in college and building a life in a city away from my family. One night, a group of about fifteen of us students, most of us women, went to a downtown bar to listen to a band and dance. We sat together at a long table.

I was dancing. I was having a great time. And then the band took a break and, as the drummer walked by me, he said, "You sure know how to shake your ass."

I went cold. I had to leave. I had my own car, but a friend offered to take me home since I looked upset. I was sure I was fine, just *fine*. I got to my apartment and I realized that my roommate was gone for the weekend.

I found every sharp knife in the kitchen, went upstairs to my bedroom, moved my dresser and a table in front of the closed door, and set the knives next to the bed and between the bed and the wall. And then I stayed awake all night, listening for intruders, my heart pounding, flinching at any sound. The next morning, I called the rape crisis center and talked with a counselor while I huddled under a table in the corner of the dining room.

I was afraid to be seen through the windows. The police had said they believed my assailant had stalked me, including window-peeping.

The drummer's smart-ass comment had reminded me that I was being seen in public in a sexual way. He could have followed me home.

It was a major trigger. But, with help, it also let some of those memory strands find their proper place. That part of me that had gone away, dissociated and numbed out, had come home.

Or so I like to think. With PTSD, you never know. I may have a whole other layer, or four, of strands that are left from that event. And I may be right back with them in an hour.

I hadn't felt a pressure for my memory strands to emerge. I couldn't have guessed that a drummer's comment would open that history. How can I predict what else might send me diving under a table? Or when?

No Tomorrow

PTSD hacks at the continuity of life and disintegrates the idea of a future.

Having PTSD is having a life narrative that is missing chapters and stops in the middle of a sentence. It's a life of cliff-hangers with no resolution at the start of the new television season.

"When last we left our heroine she was cowering under a bed." Actually, it's more likely that, the last we saw the heroine she was staring blankly at her assailant. The cowering is there and not there. The steps after the cowering are missing. As we rejoin her, she's nervously giving a speech to her eighth-grade class. Sections of the past are coherent, but much is a mosaic of memories and images that don't quite tell a story but groan and/or howl as they nudge for a place.

There are no assumptions about tomorrow, no trust that today's actions will build a platform that I can stand on tomorrow. That lack of faith is one of the gulfs I feel separates me from most other people.

For example, the 9/11 attacks didn't surprise me. Although I never would have guessed that they would happen, they weren't a surprise and I was baffled by the reaction of most Americans. They were appalled that their sense of safety had been violated. I really didn't know that so many people felt entitled to their routines, their assumptions. They were outraged.

Didn't they understand? There is no safety, no security.

Suddenly the world was completely different for them. The world can be completely different for any of us at any time. I know that in my bones. How could they not know this?

I'm not insensitive to their loss. This was obviously a traumatic experience for a vast number of people and I wouldn't wish that on anyone. I was just shocked at how many trauma virgins there are in the world.

I didn't expect people to "get over it" or "get on with it" right away. I didn't expect stoicism or personal growth. I just expected others to be more used to it.

It's actually quite similar to my reaction to friends who have lost a beloved parent. Being told that their "life will never be the same" just perplexes me.

I don't assume that life will be, much less be consistent.

But "living like there is no tomorrow" is supposed to be fun, isn't it? No tomorrow? No consequences. Be as hedonistic as you want.

That only makes sense if your today is pleasant and you want to savor it unhindered by the "what ifs" of tomorrow. If today is hell, you want out. For many people with PTSD, that can lead to what looks like irresponsible behavior. But it's not fun; it's not savored. It's escape; it's numbing. It's desperate.

❧ ❧ ❧

I've done my share of escaping and numbing, of indulging in what is now called "at risk" behavior. So what? Risk from the standpoint of someone with PTSD is evaluated entirely differently than it is for the rest of the world. The boxes in the hallway are an immediate risk. Ketchup splattered on the kitchen floor is an emergency. Sitting in a restaurant without having my back against a wall is enough of a risk to make me uneasy, but I can do it if I have to. For many combat veterans, going to bed without having a gun within reach is risky.

We're protecting ourselves *now*. The common wisdom is that we shouldn't continue some comforting (or numbing) habits because they may do things like raise our risk of cancer in 20 years. That's an abstraction. It's a left-brain fact that doesn't impact our right-brain experience. It's yet another marker that we don't quite fit in the world.

To some degree, loss is woven into my very existence. Grief is my baseline. As much as I've mourned in messy, physically painful ways, ached with sadness and gotten stuck in funks, I can't think of a single loss that has changed me or my view of the world. I'm not talking about depression but maybe a certain amount of fatalism. I feel like I've always known that horrible things can happen at any time.

ø   ø   ø

I don't assume that there will be a tomorrow. This can create a bit of a dilemma when there is.

If I survive the night, morning hands me a new card. Sometimes it is a part of a sequence that I have been organizing. Sometimes it's an additional weight added to my strained emotional carry-on. Sometimes it is completely random and makes my past feelings or efforts at continuity meaningless. But every day, I have a choice. I can accept that "Okay, this is what life is like now," and do the best I can to handle it.

Or I can kill myself.

I think of killing myself every single day. Suicidal ideation is another common component of PTSD. It also feels like one of the more dangerous ones to talk or write about because it really scares other people and, in response, they could take away some of my freedoms. They could try to control me and what I do with my body. The last thing I want is to have someone else take control of my body again.

I don't have my death planned but knowing that I have the option of killing myself has been very comforting at times. It's what has given me a choice, which has given me some sense of control over my existence.

I have had three types of suicidal thoughts. The first two are intrusive. The third is more voluntary and so, I suspect, more serious.

"I can always kill myself" has been a sort of involuntary mantra for me for most of my life. When I think of something in the future that causes a flash of panic, like the fear of missing a deadline, it's the first thought that comes to mind. There isn't supposed to be a future, so if it looks like there may be and it will scare me, I can opt out.

From my discussions with people who do not have PTSD, I understand that most people have moments of panic but they don't immediately lead to suicidal thoughts. Mine have. Such flashes of pressure back me into a corner a moment before an assailant finds that he's successfully trapped me. (Incidentally, the sides of the corner are made of the rough bare wood that gives you splinters. I have no idea where this sensation comes from. It's just another unattached strand of memory life).

I used to have the thought, "I can always kill myself," pop into my mind dozens of times a day. It still visits on most days but I'm far less anxious in general, so the visits are less frequent now.

The second type of suicidal thoughts emerged in adulthood. I have flash images of dying. The most common is that I step off a ledge, am caught at the neck by a rope strung in front of me and choke.

Other visions of dying have become intrusive visitors only at specific times. For example, when my first marriage was disintegrating (along with my image of my marriage and myself), I found it hard to empty the dishwasher. I would open the door, pull out the rack that held the knives and have a flash of grabbing a large knife and slitting my throat. It was an image that came awfully close to an impulse. Frighteningly close. If I ever kill myself, it won't be on impulse.

My third type of suicidal thought is voluntary. It's when I hurt and I want it to stop.

Everyone knows that there are different types of physical pain. A flesh wound is different from a headache and an amputation is different from a migraine. My experience is that the same is true of the pains of PTSD. There are different types and different intensities. Some pains are a nuisance, some require me to make major accommodations in my life, some can incapacitate me.

And some are so overwhelming that they eliminate everything else in the world. My life shrinks to this second. My entire nervous system is flooded with stress hormones. I am getting a constant electric shock and everything hurts. My body hurts from clenched muscles and stomach cramps. I feel punched in the chest and my throat closes. It's hard to move. My hands shake. All the loss and fear I've ever felt in life is condensed to this very moment and I can't think beyond it. Writhing in pain sounds dramatic but feels accurate. I hold on just long enough so that I can take another breath.

And I think, "I can't live like this."

But I have survived such episodes. Some were self-limiting. Others came in waves over months of misery. I think what got me through was that I remembered that I have not always had such intense pain, I sought help and I've gone on medications. Some eventually helped.

When I've shared with people that I take meds, I've often gotten reactions such as, "Aren't you afraid of the long-term effects of these drugs?" My answer is, "I have no desire to live a long, unhappy life." My real answer is, "There is no long-term."

❧ ❧ ❧

Not all PTSD pain is so obviously urgent. Sharp pain floods me but despair and hopelessness gently wash over my feet, eroding my tenuous foundation and seeping into my being. It becomes a weight in my chest and, as my feet slip, I topple into a netherworld. My ties to other times and to those I love loosen and I think, "Why bother?"

I suppose it's partly depression, but there is also a sort of existential angst documented in others with PTSD. Where is the meaning in all of this? Why live in a world this ugly?

If I'm caught in this netherworld, I don't have many emotional resources left to deal with PTSD triggers I might run into, or even everyday annoyances like broken appliances or PMS. These are the times that I've gotten closest to actually contemplating suicide, to feeling that the escape of death would be a gift.

ᘓ   ᘓ   ᘓ

I have made one suicide attempt. Although I can't say I really wanted to die, I didn't want to live anymore, either. There is actually a great distance between those two emotional points.

I was sixteen, living in my family's house, and miserable.

One night about an hour after everyone, including my father, had gone to bed, I got up and searched through my mother's drawer of pills. There was a new bottle of aspirin. She had lots of other drugs; I chose aspirin. I swallowed everything in the bottle, wrapped the bottle in a paper towel and stuffed it in the trash. Then I sat down on the basement steps and sobbed. I waited a little while and realized I was getting scared.

I quietly went up to the kitchen, got the phone, stretched the cord as far as I could, and brought it back with me to the dark steps. I called a friend and told her what I had done. While we were talking, my mother got up because she had a headache and wanted to take some aspirin. When she couldn't find the bottle, she checked to see who was in bed, realized I wasn't and started looking for me. I was sobbing on the phone to my friend, who was trying to figure out how serious this was, when my mom opened the door to the basement stairs, saw me and yelled, "Did you take all the aspirin? Where's the aspirin?"

I hung up and admitted to my mom what I had done. She called the emergency room at the hospital. The nurses on staff asked how much I had taken and how long ago. They then gave my mom a recipe for a concoction that would make me vomit. (Health care systems and liability threats have changed since then.) All I remember is that it had mustard in it. And that it worked.

I was in the half bath that was in sight of the kitchen, kneeling over the toilet heaving and sobbing. My mother had gotten my dad out of bed and he was sitting at the end of the kitchen table, positioned so he could watch me.

He started by drumming his fingers on the table and then he exploded.

"How could you do this, Marla? How could you do this to me? What if it had worked? What if you had died? What would people say about me then?"

I have had times since then when I have felt just as miserable, but never as unloved.

❧   ❧   ❧

Even in my deepest drifts of despair, my connections with other people have held enough to provide an answer to the question, "Why bother?" They have made me wonder if the gift of death to me would be worth the cost of pain to others.

So I've made a deal with myself. If I finally reach the conclusion that my life seems too painful or pointless to live, then my death shouldn't be meaningless. There are countless high-risk places in the world that need people to ease the awful living conditions of the inhabitants, people who want to live. If I don't care if I live, then I'll put myself someplace where I might be able to do some good before I get shot, someplace where the visibility of a middle-aged American citizen's death might bring some needed publicity. I've come to think of it as suicide by humanitarian effort or political strategy.

And, if I survive, if there continues to be a tomorrow, fine. I'll deal with that card then.

Ebb and Flow

Chronic doesn't mean consistent. I've had post-traumatic stress disorder for most of my life. That doesn't mean the symptoms are predictable or that my susceptibility to triggers has been constant. It depends on the moment, the day, my life stage. PTSD symptoms can lie dormant for years (as in delayed onset PTSD) or simply recede for a while, only to reemerge fiercely for no obvious reason.

Understanding the apparent randomness of PTSD is key to its treatment. There is a logic, however tangled, to one's reactions to the world. Unfortunately, diagnosis and appropriate care are often delayed for those of us without a single, obvious traumatic event that can be used to pinpoint the onset of symptoms. This was especially true before research into PTSD increased as a result of the damage done to many Vietnam War veterans.

It's obvious to me now that I had a mix of acute stress reactions and PTSD symptoms from the time I was eleven to about age fifteen. I attributed all of my personal and family problems to my mother's mental illness. My mother, siblings and I only talked about Act One in our house. The daylight and early evening hours were what we considered our family life.

Act Two, the portion of our life controlled by our father, wasn't really acknowledged. If Dad was discussed among us kids, he was seen as a bit of an oaf and a mystery, with a belligerent streak. He was compartmentalized as a weird guy who showed up and did unpredictable, sometimes mean, things.

The problem was Mom and her psychosis. Dad was just a bit player.

I made it through middle school in an emotional blender with an intermittent pulse control. I would whir through insanity, violence, protectiveness, and then stop, jumbled and immobilized, frozen in time, only to be jarred back into chaos in another unpredictable moment.

I knew there was something wrong with me and looked for help. But asking for help is always a crapshoot and can make matters much worse before they get better.

At twelve, I went to my school guidance counselor's office, told her that my mom was in the psych ward, burst into tears, and said I wanted to kill myself. With all of the psychological support available in an underfunded middle school in a small blue-collar city in 1967, I was told that the world would be a much sadder place without me and that I should wash my face before heading back to class.

But it did have an impact and I received special attention; I was given the role of audiovisual assistant at the school.

It was also about this time that, after seeing ads on television, I told my mother that I thought I needed a laxative. When she asked why in the hell would I want a laxative, I told her, "Because I think I need to relax."

She took me to the family doctor who, at that time, was also prescribing for her. He put me on antidepressants — first-generation tricyclics — that I took until I was eighteen.

I can't say if the antidepressants helped. Nobody asked. I don't know how I would have felt without them. Nevertheless, I was often miserable and I came to define myself as depressed.

I don't doubt that I was depressed, but that was not the core of my problem. As many therapists over the years would tell me, "Marla, you just don't have a depressive personality." Having done my research, I would agree. Through my tears.

Given my background, depression was not unexpected. But I was more than sad. My world was chaotic, and so were my reactions to it.

❧   ❧   ❧

Over the years, I went to counseling, and then I had more counseling. Stories of growing up with a psychotic mother provided endless paths of exploration for therapists.

However, there were stretches of time when the pieces settled enough to resemble what I believed to be stability. I was still hypervigilant. I would still startle, though less dramatically. I would still be stuck and frozen at times, but I was seldom swamped by the past. These reprieves could last for months or years.

❧ ❧ ❧

The first of the "remissions" I would have from PTSD symptoms happened in my last year of high school. The current had shifted some at home and I was around less often.

Still, I knew that I was different from most other students. Sometimes that difference showed up in social settings but, by then, I was learning to navigate those. I knew to keep quiet when everyone else indulged in routine griping about unreasonable parents.

And sometimes that difference would smack me with no warning.

I once turned in a short story in an English class. The teacher was great and gave helpful individual attention to my writing. She noted that one of my characters was behaving unrealistically by shifting from calm to rage with no warning. She told me that I needed to include a build-up to such a big emotional transition because people didn't act that way.

I was really confused, looked straight at her and said, "My father does."

She blinked, then looked at me with that unwavering intensity that I've come to realize is the result of others' trying to bridge the gulf between us and said, "That may be, but most readers won't be able to relate to that. You need to write so that the majority of readers believe what you say is possible."

It was kind. It was real. It was helpful. It identified me as living outside the mainstream but gave me a hint about how to do that.

* * *

It was during these remissions, these stretches of relative stability in my adulthood, that I found the concentration to relearn my high-school French so I could use it when working in Africa, the curiosity to study history and the creativity to develop garden designs. I've thrown myself into pottery, studied the chemistry of glazes and awakened from dreams of tile designs and colors. I've learned the botany of perennials. I've researched countries and cultures where I've worked. I've gotten lost in the texture and design of traditional textiles from around the globe.

And I did work that I loved. I drew no line between my work and personal life. My work was acting on my values. I got paid for it. What more could one ask for in life?

But these times of energy and focus always felt like a temporary gift, a timecard with an unknown expiration date. I assumed that each overseas contract I landed might be my last. I saw no career ladder, just moments of light and opportunity, savored for their challenge and the glimpse of hope and humaneness in the world.

During these times, I still lived life on a split screen, but my current life filled most of it. The montage of clips from my past continued in an uneven wavering strip off to one side, distracting but manageable.

Each morning started with the same check-in of my bruised layers, but it was a more fleeting exercise. I would continue to have my minimum daily requirement of suicidal thoughts, but they were just habit. I would still find the need to crawl into my closet at times, cowering and sobbing for no reason I could identify. But those moments would pass. I would get jumpy, edgy and irritated but gave myself enough buffer times throughout each day to sit and regroup, just in case I needed it. Sleeping at night was always a problem.

I was having relatively mild PTSD symptoms and I was managing, but I knew I wasn't free. Perhaps that's why I savored those wonderful moments. I didn't take them for granted.

Knowing that any stability I felt was transitory and not trusting that the future existed made it especially difficult to work toward concrete goals, like completing college degrees.

The image I have of these times is also drawn from the Westerns I watched on television as a kid. The Good Guy is huddled behind Rock A, avoiding the onslaught of bullets from the Bad Guys. The Good Guy's only real hope of survival is to somehow make it to Rock B. Getting to Rock B seems impossible, though. Still, he makes a dash for it and, miraculously, slides behind the safety of Rock B with perhaps only a bullet in his thigh, which he barely notices.

These self-improvement indulgences felt like times of extreme vulnerability and I rushed through them as fast as I could. I have always felt an ominous shadow just outside my range of vision. I believed that the floor could drop out from under me at any time.

And it has.

*   *   *

I've had two long-lasting episodes in my adulthood that were, at the time, diagnosed and treated as severe depression. In hindsight, the PTSD triggers are obvious to me.

The first episode was immediately after my first wedding, when two triggers snapped at once. I realized I was again legally part of a family. At the same time, I also got a new manager at work, a much older man who dismissed my work and over-managed me.

The episode lasted about six months. I had every symptom every day and long periods of that excruciating pain of living breath to breath. I would lie on my bed and cry, then sob, then howl and nearly convulse with heaving.

It was as if someone had taken the top off my box of memory strands and thrown me in. I was enveloped in a concentrated mix of intense sensations and emotions, drowning in my own existence.

The line between the past and present grew thin, too thin. I couldn't concentrate enough to read. I could hold some conversations, but I would cry randomly.

I went to a counselor who provided support while I explored why I felt so trapped. She was the first therapist who ever prodded me about the role my dad had played in my life, but I continued to see him as just an unpredictable bit player. It was my then-husband who gave me the most helpful tool, the ladder that let me climb out of the box.

He told me, "You know, if being married is so hard on you, we can get divorced and just continue our relationship. We don't have to be married."

It reminded me that I did continue to have choices and helped me separate the past from my present situation. I also changed my work situation. I found the floor beneath my feet again.

The second major episode was more than a decade later. The trigger was a delightful eleven-year-old neighborhood girl who came into my life by telling me I had pretty flowers in my yard and asking if she could help me grow them. She came by most days and I enjoyed her company. As I came to know her better, I discovered that she had a mentally ill mother, a missing abusive father, and, often, not enough to eat. At the time, I didn't realize how much she reminded me of myself at that age.

I did what I could to make sure that she and her mom got what financial and social services they could. And I worried about her. When her mother became less stable, we looked into providing her a foster home.

I felt desperate to intervene in her life or make sure someone else did. However, the family was fairly transient and they moved, first to a tent pitched in a cemetery, then somewhere out of state.

This major episode was as intense as the first but I was somewhat more prepared. I was once again dropped in the box of memory strands, I was just as overwhelmed with loss, fear and hurt, but I knew I had escaped once before. I was older and more assertive about getting care. My general practitioner prescribed one of the new antidepressants and I searched for a therapist.

❧ ❧ ❧

This led me to what I now consider a perfect example of therapists not recognizing PTSD when they see it.

I was sitting in a therapist's office during a second session with her. I was crying a lot in those days and was crying in her office. She asked about my mom and I told her that I felt she had had a hard life.

The therapist asked, "Why do you think you cry when you talk about your mom?"

I stared at her. I couldn't think of an answer. I knew I should have one, but I couldn't come up with a thing. I felt like I was in music class when I was eleven and trying to figure out when the metronome might click again. I froze and may have dissociated.

She said, "Obviously, you cry because you feel guilty. You don't seem invested enough in this process to really work on these issues at this time, so I think it's best that I not work with you as a client."

She fired me.

She exemplified Maslow's hammer. "If all you have is a hammer, everything looks like a nail."

I've experienced this often with people. I've told you that I learned to be careful whom I told about my childhood. I've also learned to brace myself if I decide to tell someone about my condition or my symptoms.

Usually I do so in an attempt to bridge that gulf between me and others, to diminish my sense of isolation. And I do it incrementally, sort of testing others' reactions to small quirks before giving them the full picture. Still, it's painful to confide in someone only to have the gulf widen instead of narrow.

"Have you tried _____?"

Many people make suggestions with the kindest of intentions and are open to understanding PTSD, to know me better.

But not all. And those others? They are adamant in their suggestions and I feel judged if I don't follow them. They are the ones who seem to need me to do something that fits their choices and their limited range of experiences. They become impatient with me if I don't immediately accept their solutions with relief. They are not open to learning more about PTSD. They don't want to know that the brain changes associated with PTSD won't be reversed solely through diet, exercise, herbs, meditation, taking or not taking certain drugs, sleep routines, full-spectrum lights, sensory deprivation tanks, colon cleansing, having my dental fillings replaced, eschewing plastics, and/or the religion of their choice.

They also live by Maslow's hammer. I can only assume that it's too difficult, too scary, to accept that a continuous state of injury is possible in their world, so they conclude it must be of my own making or due to my lack of motivation.

I feel diminished.

I suspect some combat veterans with PTSD get a certain degree of this, but those of us without a single traumatic event to "justify" our symptoms may well be considered malingerers if we don't accept a non-traumatized person's prescription for happiness; if we don't accept that someone else knows us better than we know ourselves.

This is a particularly sensitive issue for victims of child sexual abuse since it is a reinforcement of the early messages of "your feelings/perceptions don't count" and "you don't know the truth, I'll tell you what the truth is." Victims of early abuse are particularly vulnerable to those who authoritatively say, "You know what your problem is? It's _____," whether the source is a therapist, a pastor, a neighbor or a partner. Early abuse leaves us feeling confused and abandoned. We want someone to tell us what's going on, what's normal. We want the comfort of definition but, if that definition comes entirely from someone else, it's repeating the same process of shutting ourselves down and shushing that small voice that says, "But . . . I feel/want/need/see/smell/hear . . . "

It's like leaving one cult for another, even if each cult is made up of just one other person. The cult could be a commune, a country club, an academic field, a congregation, or a school of psychological thought — anything that reaches out to that free-floating anxiety and says, "Here, this is the right way to think and feel. This is what will make you happy." It's all so reassuring, as long as we can shush that little voice.

I have shushed my voice countless times as an adult and, although there has always been a cost, I have also benefited from being held within and learning about a few of these everyday cults. They did help me manage some secondary symptoms, like depression, but they were not the lifesavers they claimed to be (or I hoped they would be). They did allow me to just tread water and gain some tools for living while I defined the brink of my own undertow.

But I was lucky. They could have been anchors that sank me.

๏   ๏   ๏

A therapeutic school of thought that is so pervasive that it's almost considered common knowledge is that expressing deep painful feelings is a way to exorcise them. You "work through" the old feelings, which allows them to dissipate, leaving you with all the excess energy that had been used to suppress the feelings.

I think of this as the "lance the abscess" school of thought. "It ain't pretty and it hurts like hell, but you'll feel so much better after it heals." This process works well for some people with repressed pain from life circumstances, and it certainly helped me with parts of my past.

But it's not a cure-all and has its limits for those of us with PTSD. This is because the pain associated with trauma is not simply repressed. It's not an abscess lying under the skin. It's deeply embedded in the circuitry of the nervous system and brain. Outside attempts to dig deeper, find that sore spot and evoke the emotions associated with it may work, but they won't help. Instead of releasing toxins that allow for healing, that well-intentioned lance acts as a conduit for an electric shock. The pain is relived, but not relieved. Often, the traumatized person is, in fact, retraumatized.

So, the therapist who fired me? She was wrong about my level of investment, but right about our not working together. It was a very bad fit. The gift I got from her, however, was a recommendation for a psychiatrist, upon request.

❡   ❡   ❡

I had always been adamantly opposed to seeing a psychiatrist. I wasn't my mother. I might sob and shake while hiding in a closet, I might go away sometimes, I might hit the floor when something clanged in the kitchen, but I knew I wasn't the Virgin Mary, damn it!

But I was desperate. I wanted my life back, no matter how fragile it might be.

The psychiatrist I saw was great. We did some talk therapy along with an assessment of my psychophysical state. He
didn't diagnose me with PTSD (or at least he never told me if
he suspected it) but he did educate me about brain function
and explained, gently, that much of what I was experiencing
was probably "hard-wired" by that point. He was the first
to suggest that my sleep issues were so long-standing that
they could now be a part of my brain stem functioning and it
might be unrealistic to expect to be free of all my symptoms.
However, I could learn to live with them better.

Okay. That was a different perspective. I wasn't going to
be cured and free but then no one was asking me to drink
the Kool-Aid again, either.

I felt like he was on my side and was optimistic about
finding a good balance of drugs to get me back on track. I
remember my moment of glory when I did start to feel like I
had my life back. I cleaned and organized the storage shed.
It was a triumph.

ø   ø   ø

And I balanced. The demons slunk back. My life returned, with its quirks and moments of inexplicable panic in
more manageable doses.

I saw myself differently, though. I no longer defined myself as simply depressed, which I viewed as the result of
thinking patterns and repressed feelings. I saw that I was
more complicated and that my symptoms were beyond the
control of thoughts alone. This made sense to me because

so many of my reactions occurred before my conscious brain ever engaged.

That had been one of the voices I had shushed. On some level, I always knew that I couldn't just think my way out of these floods of emotion and irrational behavior. I knew that my sequencing was different than that.

However, if accepting that I couldn't consciously control (or emotionally "work through") all my symptoms was freeing, it was also humbling.

I had, in fact, survived my childhood and being raped. More often than not, I function quite well. In those ways, I am a survivor.

But I am left with something else, something lasting, something from which it is not so easy to "move on."

Flood

Facing the trauma of child abuse is hard. So hard, in fact, that often the perpetrator has to die before it becomes possible. Only then is the world safe enough to let the truth surface.

That was true for me.

My dad died the summer I was forty-eight. I already was having a tough time. I was in the middle of getting a divorce that, though amicable, was very painful. I was living in a city that was still relatively new to me and I was unsure about the job I had moved there for. I felt somewhat depressed and had found a therapist. My closest friends and support system were hours away and I isolated myself from them at times.

One friend called and left a voice mail. "Hey, you don't seem to be answering your emails. I can think of three possible reasons this might be: A) You're extremely busy with work you enjoy and don't have time for personal emails. That would be acceptable. B) You're having a really good time with friends in the area and don't have time for personal emails. That would be acceptable. Or C) you're really depressed, are spending hours playing Spider Solitaire on your computer and are ignoring your personal emails. That would not be acceptable. Let me know what's going on."

I emailed back, "Or D) my dad died and I'm busy cleaning the pornography out of his apartment."

He wrote, "You can always top me, can't you?"

🌢 🌢 🌢

For the record, it's not easy to get rid of pornography from an apartment in a senior citizen housing complex. I discovered that you can't just toss it in the trash because other tenants go Dumpster-diving at night whenever someone has died and the family is cleaning up.

At the time, my dad's death seemed remarkably unremarkable. All of us kids had distanced ourselves emotionally, although most of us had made some effort to ease his financial situation to some degree. His death brought us together physically for the first time in more than a decade.

Relationships among us were strained as adults but we actually got along quite well during the day and a half we spent cleaning his apartment. We were a united front against his weirdness and our past. We puzzled over the forty-two bottles of shampoo he had stockpiled and sighed over the collection of unused gift cards we had sent him.

There were also a lot of "remember this?" moments, although few were followed by stories or laughter. Most just focused our eyes on a single item and we silently felt the bond of being the only people in the world who knew its meaning.

His funeral was a private service and only some of us were willing to say a few words. The oldest simply said, "Well, he was a pretty good dad until I was about eight."

After the service, one of my siblings and I decided to go to the bar where he routinely met his drinking buddies. This was his social life. We knew that his favorite bar changed over time but the maintenance staff at his apartment complex told us where he had been going for happy hour beer specials every day for the last couple of years.

We entered the darkened bar, walked up to the bartender and told her who we were. She didn't really look at us but said that she had heard our dad had died and he had been part of what everyone called the "Old-Timers' Club," the old guys who only came in for the daily discount specials and always sat together at the end of the bar.

She introduced us to the one old-timer who was there.

He looked at us and said, "So he was your dad, huh?"

"Yup."

He fiddled with his napkin, took a gulp of his draft beer, then looked straight at us and said, "I'm not gonna lie to you kids. Your father was an asshole."

We stayed for a little while, each had a drink and listened to stories. When it came time to pay, we dug through our wallets to find as much cash as we could. We put $120 in the general tip jar and asked the bartender to share it with the waitresses who were usually there at happy hour. I don't even care if she kept all of it for herself. Over the last year and a half, she had spent more time with our dad than we had. She earned it.

🌢　🌢　🌢

The aftermath of a parent's death can be messy no matter how irrelevant he or she has been in your day-to-day life. The image I have is of parents acting as bookends, holding a series of books, the kids and the assumptions about family structure, in a reliable order. When one parent falls, it causes a jolt and not always, but often, the order shifts. Things slip. The underlying cohesiveness of "siblinghood in this family" sort of falls apart. Some kids find themselves becoming the missing bookend, trying to keep order, but there is slippage. Some fall off the shelf, leaving those remaining awkwardly upright but not supported. Things aren't right, as they should be, among those left.

My mom had died about twenty years earlier, after spending three years in a care facility. At the time, I saw my siblings and me as a band of musketeers. We had survived and it was one for all and all for one. But that wasn't real. Some immediately recreated the divisive patterns my mother had had with specific siblings.

So, that bookend was partially replaced, although the real weight of it — our shared concern for Mom's care — was gone. But there were now gaps among the books. We were all adults living very separate lives, only occasionally tilting toward one another for tentative support. But we stayed on the bookshelf, united mostly by our need to lean away from the remaining bookend and our confusion about what, if anything, we owed it.

When my father died, both bookends were gone, as was the shelf itself. I had really wanted to hold the collection together. My sibs were my family. We had a shared history that no one else understood. Even though it was no longer part of my daily life, caring for and protecting the others had been an organizing principle in my emotional life, just as caring for my mother had. It had given my life an under-lying structure.

What I hadn't realized is that it had also provided the structure for my box of shit. It was the emotional rationale for separating and isolating all of those memory strands. How could I indulge in my own feelings when others need-ed protection and oversight? Just as I had tucked away my anger at my mom for intruding into my life after she was released from the psych ward, I tucked away my wants and fears to protect my siblings.

The sibling cohesiveness after my father's funeral last-ed about thirty-six hours. Then it exploded and dissipated for good.

❧ ❧ ❧

Over the course of the next year, I realized that sacrifice on my part did not necessarily mean gain for anyone else and that giving is often unnoticed. If it is recognized, it may actually be resented as intrusion. However, I had needed to be a caretaker. I saw it as my job. Focusing my attention on others helped me believe I was safer, out of the line of fire. I was a medic, not the infantry.

When my father died, I lost the family caretaker job that I thought I had. And, much like the WWII veterans who had functioned fairly well until they retired, the loss of that role precipitated a collapse. The sides of the pretty box of shit that I had been dragging with me my entire life began to disintegrate.

I mourned the loss of that box more than I had mourned either of my parents' deaths. As much as it had slowed me down, that false structure and safety had comforted me more than either of them had.

I mourned it and the story it had told me about who I was. I mourned my wasted, pointless efforts and, justified or not, I felt the stab of ingratitude. I mourned the loss of my siblings as I had known them.

And, as I grieved, the cotton string that had held the box to me also disintegrated. I was free, but had no idea who "I" was, if not a caretaker.

Then the box's contents, all those disconnected strands of memory — the smells, the emotions, the sensations of my past experiences — began to float freely. They were loose, yet circled about me like a hurricane in slow motion. Instead of dragging a box, I sought the center, ever shrinking, calm of the storm.

🝀 🝀 🝀

Unlike the depressive episodes that dropped me into the box, isolating me and engulfing me with emotion and sensation, at this point the strands entered my life. Contact with the circling strands could cause anything to happen. A food would suddenly repulse me. Music and television irritated; they were too much stimulation. I sobbed at inexplicable times and then snapped back to ordering my life with brittle smugness.

Then I started having flashbacks in my therapy sessions. I went to the times and places that had been described in the small handwritten narratives on the sides of the box. I knew all of these things had happened. I had always been able to describe them. But I hadn't felt them.

Suddenly, I did. In the present. *NOW.* I felt my throat close, pressure on my chest and the panic of suffocating as my dad once again slammed me against the wall. I felt myself gag, trying not to vomit as he forced me to eat. I felt my stomach clench and body stiffen as I heard his car pull into the driveway after the bars closed.

And I felt terror.

Admitting to myself that I was afraid of my dad, feeling that fear and powerlessness, was overwhelming. I was drowning in it.

Then I started having flashbacks in other settings. Kitchen splatters that had always made me tense sent me cowering and sobbing into corners.

My startle response grew. Before, a dropped dish might have made me jump higher than most people. Now I screamed and covered my face before I realized I had done so.

I had a hard time concentrating and often couldn't read. I just didn't remember sentences long enough to have full paragraphs make sense to me.

I was diagnosed with post-traumatic stress disorder and began to learn about it. I was prescribed appropriate drugs by a psychiatrist who also worked with veterans.

❧ ❧ ❧

Frankly, at first PTSD seemed a little overdramatic for my situation. I hadn't been in combat. Yes, I had been raped as an adult, but that's not what I was feeling now, what I was remembering.

The version of our family's story that I learned went like this: Mom was crazy. We didn't have much money, but weren't supposed to let anyone know we were poor. Dad wasn't around much, which was good because he was just weird. In whispers, we would say that Dad was an alcoholic and sometimes got belligerent. But it wasn't *that* bad. After all, as my father used to proudly remind me, he had never hit one of us with a closed fist.

The word "abuse" was never used and I had never applied it to my family situation, even though I had studied abuse and worked in the field of domestic violence for a time. I had learned models and ideas that helped me make sense of the world, but not my experience in it. The split between my intellectual knowledge and my personal emotional awareness was stunningly effective.

But I was not living my life intellectually at this point. The past side of my split-screen life came close to wiping out the current side. I did recover memories, but nothing was a surprise. Most are simply extensions of the events I had described on the outside of my pretty box of shit. Others were like unwrapping a stored Christmas ornament.

"Oh yeah, and then there's that one."

The baseline of my existence was emotionally exhausting. The spikes in anxiety from flashbacks and triggers felt almost intolerable.

And, as an adult, I had never considered myself an anxious person. Depressed? Yes? Anxious? No? I had been the one looking for adventure and stimulation. I hadn't realized that I was also looking for something to break through my numbness.

Well, I wasn't numb anymore.

I took anti-anxiety drugs to help push the past side of my split-screen life over enough to function in the current side of my world on a basic level. (Still, there was that exaggerated startle incident in the grocery check-out line.)

The drugs also helped me focus enough to read. If I could engage my intellect, it gave my emotions a rest. So, when I wasn't incapacitated by emotions, or exhausted from staying in the present just enough to work, I studied trauma and PTSD.

I couldn't accept this diagnosis, this "answer," without doing my own research. It made sense. It explained why the world and my reactions to it seemed so random at times. Understanding it intellectually made it easier for me to accept it and, in turn, feel its reality.

The traumatic pain that is embedded in my nervous system began to surface on its own.

The first time I really felt my child-level terror of my father, I thought it would kill me. I was swamped with adrenaline and thought, "I can't live like this."

I could only take it in small doses. I remember gardening that summer, and stopping, breathing and deciding to allow myself to *feel* it. I would remember him standing over me, get a flash of overwhelming terror and then think, "Okay, that's enough." It was my way of checking to see if it had been "really all *that* bad." For me, it had.

Feeling the terror in measured amounts also helped desensitize me to it. Sort of.

Understanding PTSD and its role in my life was a lot like my experience as a toddler when I was finally tall enough to see what was on the table. I could begin to see what were triggers for me. Fewer of them were just random items coming into view.

But coming to understand the biology of long-standing PTSD also meant giving up the hope that I would ever be completely free of it. I can't self-actualize myself out of this haunted house.

I can only learn to live in it more comfortably.

Living Anyway

It has been seven years since my father died; I've had seven birthdays of my own, celebrating my existence without feeling the shadow of his.

I no longer drag the weight of my box of shit and I walk more comfortably in my own skin. My stride is a bit longer, my pace more even.

But I am not free, not as I had imagined freedom. I thought freedom meant my past would settle behind me like so much dust, that each day would be new, that I would live life on a single, current screen. Like I imagine most people do.

But every wakening still has its hesitation. Every morning starts with a streak of my most vulnerable past moments. There are no brand new days.

The box that held my memory threads is gone, but the threads are still here. They hover about me and sometimes swirl. I move, they move with me.

I have not escaped the intrusiveness of my past and no longer believe that's possible. I continue to live a split-screen life, the present on one side, the past on the other, the line between them always moving.

My past still overwhelms my present at times, but not as often as it once did and it doesn't seem to last as long. I understand it better, which helps, and I am learning to live with it.

I am generally calmer now that my memory threads are floating freely. I don't worry about corralling them and minding the box. I am more comfortable with them brushing against me. Most have become familiar. Some have even been reunited with their reference postcards and set aside. They are real, available, but not usually intrusive. The breezes of day-to-day living lift them at times and they waft about, sometimes harmlessly, sometimes smacking me in the face, briefly taking me to another time and place. They may still be random, but they're no longer a complete mystery. That alone eases the fright.

The loose threads of my memory life are just that, loose. Fresh ones, those that are raw and urgent, occasionally lash me, yanking me into pain, but most are just unexplained repeat visitors. I don't know how to introduce them but I also know that they're not likely to stay around for very long. They're random and confusing but, in general, less upsetting just because they're more familiar. And I know they will pass.

I can still be flooded with fear at any moment by everyday items or sensations. Dropped dishes can make me gasp.

Splatters and clutter in the hallway push my anxiety up, but it varies in intensity, from irritation to a need to escape. Evenings are tenser than the rest of my day; I'm more likely to get edgy in the kitchen than any other part of the house. Sleeping at night remains an issue.

This is all part of my "messiness," my imperfection, my quirkiness, my absence from the present, and proof that I am not the person I wanted to be, the person I thought I had to be.

This is a blow to my self-image. I really prefer to think of myself as someone who can deal with anything, a powerful woman who would fight off or outsmart a rapist, someone who can protect others from pain, someone who can snuff out cigarette butts with her bare feet. I don't like knowing that I am someone who cowers and apologizes when a glass breaks in the kitchen. But I am.

❧ ❧ ❧

Making peace with this has not been easy. Like many people with PTSD, I sometimes organize the world into over-simplified categories: The good and the bad, the safe and the risky, the strong and the wimpy. Logically, I know that there is a spectrum but, emotionally, I can be quite stubborn about the world's rights and wrongs. Or, more specifically, about my rights and wrongs, my smugness and my shame.

Intellectually, I know there aren't many circumstances that require snuffing out cigarettes barefoot. I also know that I add a great deal to the world as an individual and a professional by caring, listening, speaking my truth and by sharing my knowledge, my analysis, my questions. I know this because I've seen results of my contributions. I have also had others confirm this.

But that confidence can be wiped out by a single horrified cower that happens before I know its trigger. My emotional logic is: If I cringe, then I can be made to cringe. And if I can be made to cringe, any apparent strength is a facade.

At those moments, I get snagged into all-or-nothing thinking and it takes a while to shake myself free again.

Reconciling the ends of that spectrum — that I cringe *and* that I am capable — has been a struggle. In fact, it has caused me actual physical discomfort. I once sat with both hands in front of me, palms up, as if each were holding a concept of me. "I am weak, humiliated and shamed" was in one hand and "I can act on my own and others' behalf" was in the other. Trying to hold both of these ideas in my mind at the same time felt like learning advanced statistical regression in grad school. My brain hurt. I could almost feel my gray matter being forced into new folds to create a space big enough to store both ideas, that I am not invincible AND that I am not completely powerless, together.

I'm learning this, enough to live more comfortably. Enough to live anyway.

My baseline anxiety, which I had never even identified until my box disintegrated, is much lower than it has ever been. I sense my limits, though. Keeping myself afloat means recognizing that fragile barrier, the surface tension, between minding my messiness and engaging in the world, between defending myself and acting to make a difference.

❧ ❧ ❧

It is a constant balancing act. Do I stay in a triggering situation and work at desensitizing myself since it seems that "normal" people are handling it? Or . . . is it a tough situation for everyone and I just don't have the same emotional reserves or patience? Can I just say, "Screw it," and leave the situation, believing I can achieve more by putting my effort somewhere else? Or does that make me a wimp? What if I just don't want to deal with it anymore?

Do I continue to interact with someone who is as dismissive of me as my father because we're family, hoping I can find a connection that lasts? Do I just maintain the illusion of closeness even if it is a trigger? Or do I deflect and invest my caring and attention elsewhere?

What is "me" and what is my PTSD? Does it matter?

This is why I cannot think of myself as a survivor of chronic post-traumatic stress disorder. I've survived child abuse and rape, but not this. Chronic PTSD takes constant awareness, much like diabetes, and an acceptance of the random, much like epilepsy. These are conditions you live with; you don't "survive" them and move on. With chronic PTSD, there is no returning to a mindless default mode, a comfort zone, because you know too much to let that happen. So the question isn't "How do I get over this?" It's "How do I live with this knowledge?"

For me, it helps to have really low expectations of how happy I'll ever be and then savor anything above that. It's like living in Seattle and having the occasional sunny day. In this sense, I think I have an advantage over those who developed PTSD as adults. I don't have an idealized past. I never lived in San Diego. I used to live in Siberia. Seattle is fine. I can live with rain.

Since I've always had a foreshortened sense of the future, I've also never had an idealized "someday." I never sat in Siberia dreaming of Florida. I just knew I had to get out.

I don't think my approach to life is particularly negative. I think it's realistic, because I know that something horrible CAN happen at any time. The odds of that happening are smaller than they were when I was growing up, but that guarantees nothing about the next moment.

And, in my current life, that's what I have. Moments. Lots and lots of moments. Some are horrors, some are delights. Most fall somewhere in between. I'm never quite sure what's coming up next, but I'm fairly sure of the range. It isn't assured safety but it's close enough for me to live more comfortably.

I also know that each of these moments will pass. That's important, especially when I'm miserable or thinking of death. I'm positive enough to believe such moments will pass and don't define them as the "bad place where I always end up," which would mean that whatever pleasures I felt since the last bad moments were just false hope.

It's not all or nothing. It's not all or nothing. It's not all or nothing. Right?

❧ ❧ ❧

My past moments have haunted me, but they have also guided me. They have shaped my interests and my work. My emotional reactions have sent me to hell, but they have also sent me on intellectual quests. Power fascinates me and I've studied its role in organizations, management and social policy. I am acutely aware of oppression. It infuriates me from afar but can trigger me if it's too close. I tend to work in the middle somewhere.

I also know that my habit of scanning groups for small shifts in mood, developed as a defense in my family, is still with me. In fact, it has helped me be a better group leader and teacher.

And there is a reason I've been self-employed for much of my adult life. I don't deal well with authority figures. I just don't. Most people who were sexually abused as kids don't.

Consciously or not, I've made room for my messiness in my work. My relationships now have to make room for it, too.

I am remarried and have a new family. My second marriage did not trigger the "trapped" feelings I had after my first wedding. That's because the memory thread "trapped" is no longer crammed into my beautiful box of shit and I did not become immersed in it. Instead, the sense of being trapped circles about me daily with other sensations, not necessarily touching me, but never far away. Sometimes it brushes me and I pulse with momentary panic. Sometimes it makes everyday items (like boxes in a hallway) menacing. Other times, it just floats near; I notice it, and it is gone.

My current family knows this about me and accepts the intrusion of my memory threads as a part of me. They're my quirks. When I have low-level reactions, they humor me and I can laugh at myself. Beyond a certain point, however, everyone takes my reactions seriously because I'm on the verge of being sucked into the dark.

A bottle of ketchup splatters on the kitchen floor. My spouse knows it's just processed tomatoes. On some level, so do I. And, sometimes, that's all it is. And sometimes, it's a bit more and he tells me "Get out of here, Jumpy" so he can clean it up. And sometimes, it's still more and he walks with me to another room and stays close while I explode and calm. He becomes that sliver of my current life that holds firm on the screen while the past half of my life surges.

And later, he goes back to the kitchen, cleans the gluey mess from the floor, clears clutter that I might notice but he normally would not, and removes any boxes that may be in the hallways. These are things that don't matter to him but he understands what they mean to me, especially when my emotional reserves are low.

He isn't constantly scanning the landscape for my personal landmines. His life isn't dedicated to keeping me in a bubble, but he's pretty good at first aid when I need it.

But what if I dropped the ketchup when I was home alone? I know that when I lived by myself, things like that were just a pain in the ass. If I were stressed before the splatter, I might retreat to the bathroom, lock the door, shake and hyperventilate for a bit. Occasionally, such small triggers would send me cowering to the closet. But I would eventually move on and clean it up, with no apologies.

I know I can do that. I know I can calm myself. But it is incredibly comforting to share my life with someone who has a sense of what this means to me, who doesn't dismiss my emotional reality (as irrational as it is) at the very time I apologize for it, and goes so far as to rearrange the physical world to better calm me at those moments.

I don't need it for survival, but it makes life better. It's a gift, but it's a gift that was only available to me after I made room for my own messiness. How can someone help calm me if I hide my desire for it?

And my messiness doesn't mean the same thing to him as it does to me. I spent years seeing it as a fatal flaw to be hidden or exorcised. He sees it as an inextricable part of me, part of my biological package.

He's a natural scientist who works with wildlife. He just assumes that all living beings are actually mixed biological packages. If you move raccoons from Florida to Virginia, you also move raccoon rabies over state lines. Humans have mites that live in our eyebrows. Nothing is isolated unless it's in a lab. He sees personalities in the same light. We're all mixed packages and, to him, my quirks are just part of me as a package. And he feels I'm a pretty good package and am a good partner, quirks and all.

This gives me a different metaphor to make sense of my extremes and it helps. It's not black or white, hero or wimp. It's more complex than that.

* * *

In many ways, I do feel like a different person than I was seven years ago because the focus of my life is no longer a box crammed full of shit. My focus is my internal life, which is full of curiosity, caring, haunted hallways and trigger points; and my external life, which is full of mystery, beauty, wonderful people, ugliness, cruelty and triggers. My life is more complicated than it was. I have to live with dualities, mixed packages.

And yet, I am very much who I have always been. I *am* a caretaker; I want to nurture a kinder world and am sustained by the warmth and excitement of others who share that sentiment. Some of those others are my students, past and present, who engage in thoughtful dialogue and have the energy and commitment to face the tensions of the world. Some are the organizational and community leaders I've met who plod forward, with humor, despite daily temptations to just stay home and watch television or garden. And they remind me that the world is much bigger than my momentary hells and heavens.

There is work to do and I want to be a part of it.

But I feel my limits. Yes, I can facilitate high-conflict meetings. I can find that calm, accepting and analytical part of me that used to talk to my mother when she was wandering in a different reality from mine. I can accept that people have different realities and attempt to find the parts that are shared.

However, doing so is harder than it was. I used to leave such meetings and come home, put my feet up, have a glass of wine and cram whatever fear or loneliness the conflict rustled into my box of shit.

Now I nap, in the safe daylight hours. I don't necessarily sleep, but I lie quietly. I actually think of nothing without thinking of a blank sheet. And I twitch. Until I calm, which may take hours. And then I wonder if it's worth it. Do I have to do something just because I can? What if I just want to work in the garden?

❦ ❦ ❦

I live two lives at once on a split screen. I've told you that. Four hours of current life may take eight hours of my energy if I'm containing the encroachment of my past even as I talk with you.

But you don't see that. Why would you? I function well enough that my wounds are usually invisible in public.

Or, at the end of those four hours, I could feel damn near perky. When my past retreats to that vibrant strip along the edge of my screen, narrow and near but not intrusive, I have room to play or learn or teach on the current side. The present side. I can be more present. It's not complete freedom, but it's as close to it as I think I'm ever going to get. And it's wonderful.

You may sense me savoring it as we banter. Others have. I've been told by numerous people in different settings that I seem like a particularly open, happy person. And I am. Sometimes.

It's all me, it's just not all of me.

Perhaps I should be happy about "passing" so well, but I'm not. It's unsettling. Around those who trigger me, it's fine; I would rather stay cloaked. But the rest of you, the majority of you? I feel like I'm lying by omission.

So, what's my choice? If I've only known you for a while and you ask, "So, how *are* you?" and I sense you want to know me better, do I tell you about my pillowcase full of knives? If that's what's on the top of my emotional list and I don't say anything about it, then I'm pushing against the past side of my split screen with you. I will need time to recover because it sucks the life out of me.

Do I take each of you out for a beer or a walk and tell you my story? Is it all of me or only-my-public self? I find myself facing either/or social situations at the same time that I struggle to accept a both/and world.

Is there a way for me to incrementally tell you I have PTSD when you have seen few signs of it? Is there a way to easily introduce the subject when I don't have a single traumatic event that would explain my symptoms, my reality?

I didn't think so. And maybe you would rather not know anyway. Both the cause and effect are ugly. Who wants to look for those things?

I struggle with "How do I tell you?" but I also struggle with "Why don't you see it?"

Felt isolation is a symptom of PTSD, but that doesn't mean the individual with the condition generates it alone. The barriers to recognizing trauma and integrating its lasting effects into our social fabric are real. Doing so would challenge that collective comfort zone.

So I squeezed my experience into the written word in hopes of being better seen.

This is not a memoir because it is not about the past. This is about my everyday. And your everyday. And when you are finished reading this, you can take a deep breath, turn the page, and move on.

But remember that I can't do that. It's always with me, even now.

And I hope that makes you just a little less comfortable, enough to put you in range of seeing more of me and others like me.

Because we're everywhere.

Resources

Information:

- Medlineplus, a service of the U.S. National Library of Medicine and the National Institutes of Health (NIH) *http://www.nlm.nih.gov/medlineplus/posttraumatic-stressdisorder.html*

- The Posttraumatic Stress Disorder (PTSD) Alliance *http://www.ptsdalliance.org/home.html*

Online support:

- Gift From Within: An International Nonprofit Organization for Survivors of Trauma and Victimization *http://www.giftfromwithin.org/*

- PTSD Forum-Post Traumatic Stress Disorder Community *http://www.ptsdforum.org/*

Acknowledgments

I want to thank the dear friends, special family members, respected colleagues and remarkable professionals who have walked close with me in life and were midwives for this book. You are deeply, deeply appreciated.

About the Author

Marla Handy, Ph.D., has over 25 years of experience consulting with nonprofit and community organizations in the areas of strategic planning, governance and managerial development, and has worked domestically and in South America, Africa, Asia, the South Pacific, Eastern Europe and the former Soviet Union. She recently retired from teaching at a large university.

Printed in the USA
CPSIA information can be obtained
at www.ICGtesting.com
LVHW041252140124
768961LV00003B/415